The Humanist Ulrich von Hutten

UNC | COLLEGE OF ARTS AND SCIENCES
Germanic and Slavic Languages and Literatures

From 1949 to 2004, UNC Press and the UNC Department of Germanic & Slavic Languages and Literatures published the UNC Studies in the Germanic Languages and Literatures series. Monographs, anthologies, and critical editions in the series covered an array of topics including medieval and modern literature, theater, linguistics, philology, onomastics, and the history of ideas. Through the generous support of the National Endowment for the Humanities and the Andrew W. Mellon Foundation, books in the series have been reissued in new paperback and open access digital editions. For a complete list of books visit www.uncpress.org.

The Humanist Ulrich von Hutten
A Reappraisal of his Humor

THOMAS W. BEST

UNC Studies in the Germanic Languages and Literatures
Number 61

Copyright © 1969

This work is licensed under a Creative Commons CC BY-NC-ND license. To view a copy of the license, visit http://creativecommons.org/licenses.

Suggested citation: Best, Thomas. *The Humanist Ulrich von Hutten: A Reappraisal of his Humor.* Chapel Hill: University of North Carolina Press, 1969. DOI: https://doi.org/10.5149/9781469657103_Best

Library of Congress Cataloging-in-Publication Data
Names: Best, Thomas W.
Title: The humanist Ulrich von Hutten: A reappraisal of his humor / by Thomas W. Best.
Other titles: University of North Carolina Studies in the Germanic Languages and Literatures ; no. 61.
Description: Chapel Hill : University of North Carolina Press, [1969] Series: University of North Carolina Studies in the Germanic Languages and Literatures. | Includes bibliographical references.
Identifiers: LCCN 75631790 | ISBN 978-1-4696-5709-7 (pbk: alk. paper) | ISBN 978-1-4696-5710-3 (ebook)
Subjects: Hutten, Ulrich von, 1488-1523 — Humor. | Dialogues, Latin (Medieval and modern) — History and criticism. | Latin wit and humor, Medieval and modern — History and criticism. | Humanists — Germany. | Germany — Intellectual life — 16th century.
Classification: LCC PA8535 .B38 1969 | DCC 836/ .4

PREFACE

The following study is a revision of my doctoral dissertation accepted at Indiana University in June 1965. For the advice which they wisely and generously gave me during the preparation of the dissertation I would like to thank Professors Frank G. Ryder, Frank G. Banta, John P. Houston, and Eberhard Reichmann of Indiana University, along with Professor William A. Little of the University of Virginia, who encouraged me to have the study published. I wish to express my gratitude as well for financial assistance granted by the University of Virginia.

TWB

CONTENTS

I. INTRODUCTION 1
II. THE EPISTOLAE OBSCURORUM VIRORUM 6
III. HUTTEN'S USE AND APPRECIATION OF JOCULARITY 22
IV. HUTTEN'S IRONIC SATIRE 32
V. HUTTEN'S USE OF CARICATURE 44
VI. CONCLUSION 74
APPENDIX: THE PREFACE TO HUTTEN'S EDITION OF DE DONATIONE CONSTANTINI 76
NOTES 83
BIBLIOGRAPHY 96
INDEX 99

I. INTRODUCTION

The humor[1] of the humanistic knight Ulrich von Hutten (1488-1523), who was one of the most satirical members of one of Germany's most satirical generations, has not been given adequate, accurate consideration. Hutten has had great appeal in the past two-hundred years for students of the German Renaissance and Reformation. He was an intriguing and pathetic figure, a tragic Don Quixote. He has been one of Germany's most ardent patriots, admired by his country's nationalists from Herder's day to Hitler's. If he failed to alter the course of the political history of his nation, he did influence the development of its literature. For these reasons, and because his complete works have been easily accessible in an excellent edition,[2] he has received a great deal of scholarly attention, but almost none of this attention has been concerned with his humor. Albert Bauer has attempted to analyze Hutten's satire in comparison to Lucian's, but his discussion of the subject is imprecise,[3] and those few who have broached the larger matter of Hutten's handling of the comic in general have contented themselves with a glib sentence or two, usually basing their remarks on his supposed contributions to the well-known satirical work of the day, the *Epistolae obscurorum virorum* (to be referred to subsequently in this study as the *Eov*). As we shall see, many of the letters in this satire which have been ascribed to Hutten may not have been written by him at all, making even more questionable those pronouncements on his humor which were promulgated largely in connection with the *Eov*.

The idea of a more detailed presentation of Hutten's humor is implicit in the inadequacy of comment which has been made so far. The initial impetus toward a consideration of this subject, however, came from a suggestion in Robert Herndon Fife's article "Ulrich von Hutten as a Literary Problem."[4] "Hutten's type of humor is, indeed, worthy of special study," Fife states. "It has something of the quality of the Baroque comedy, where Thalia accompanies her characters with a distortion of the visage rather than an indulgent smile of superiority. A certain austerity can be noted in Hutten, even in *Nemo*, where he bases on a literary tradition of folklike humor."[5] Fife's recommendation proves to be a valid one, although Hutten's humor does not deserve study as some kind of oddity. It warrants our consideration as a neglected and partially misunderstood aspect of his art and of his personality. To show what sort of attention has been given his humor, previous comments on it follow. Because of similarity to more recent opinions, an observation of one of Hutten's contemporaries, Justus Menius, is to be cited first.

Writing to Crotus Rubeanus in 1532, Menius implied that Hutten was more a mere polemicist than a true satirist, explaining that in the *Eov* Crotus's ridicule had been much more effective than Hutten's: "Your Obscure Men had more tooth and nail than all the others, and Hutten, who was a man of outstanding eloquence and almost divine facility in poetry and outdid you in that genre, could not be considered very witty, charming, or elegant when it came to biting Cardinals and Bishops, to reviling the Papists."⁶ For fourhundred years Menius's sentiment has been shared by fellow critics in attempting to distinguish between Crotus's and Hutten's contributions to the *Eov*, and, by extension, in attempting to characterize their satire, and even Hutten's humor, in general. Hutten is described as acrid, vindictive, and reformatory, while Crotus is said to be playful, good-natured, and more sophisticated.

Most of the few remarks on Hutten's humor tend to be grounded in discussion of those same satiric epistles. The following statement, for instance, from David Friedrich Strauß's biography, is contained in his chapter entitled *"Die Epistolae obscurorum virorum."* It is, as one would assume, made primarily in reference to that work, although not exclusively, so that it does have value for us here. (Curiously enough, it also follows upon a presentation of Menius's letter.) "Für sich war er [Hutten], auch als Schriftsteller, ernster, pathetischer gestimmt," says Strauß. "Alles von Hutten, auch seine Satire, spornt zur Tat, nie vergißt er, daß man das Dumme und Schlechte nicht bloß belachen, sondern bekämpfen muß."⁷ Earlier in his book Strauß also uses the following wording of essentially the same idea: "Bei Hutten, so wie er später sich entwickelte, war dem Verkehrten gegenüber das Lachen nicht das Letzte, sondern der Zorn. Er sah in den Mißbräuchen, die er verspottete, nicht bloß das Törichte, sondern mehr noch das Verderbliche."[8] Like later critics such as Walther Brecht and Aloys Bömer, Strauß held Crotus to have been the man who loved laughter for its own sake; Hutten, to have wielded it like a sword.

As for Brecht specifically, he states in his book on the *Eov*: "Er [Hutten] war überhaupt kein geborener Künstler. Gerade in den Eov II kann man sehen, wie sehr ihm wenigstens im komischen Fach jene ruhige Sachlichkeit, die gerade in Fragen der Technik den Künstler charakterisiert, abging; Crotus, der soviel kleinere Mensch, besaß sie."[9] Here Hutten's ability is belittled excessively, though it is true that he shows at times a regrettable lack of restraint in his satire by lapsing into coarse invective, as we shall have occasion to observe.

In addition to these comments by Fife, Strauß, and Brecht, there are only two others which demand attention here. The first is a very brief utterance by Heinrich Grimm.[10] "Tiefster Ernst steht hinter seinem Lachen," Grimm says, referring to Hutten's humor in general, though with particular emphasis on *Nemo*. The second remark is by Otto Flake, who was not ashamed to announce: "Die Frage nach dem Humor Huttens kann nun endgültig beantwortet werden." Flake's answer: "Er [Hutten's humor] ist nicht fromm und seelisch wie der eigentliche deutsche, sondern angreiferisch und vibrierend, spielerisch und gefährlich in einem. Dafür ist er auch nicht gesetzt, sondern jung."[11] It will be seen that Grimm and Flake are in essential agreement with Fife, Strauß, and

INTRODUCTION

Brecht in being blinded by negative or extreme aspects of Hutten's humor, such as anger, vehemence, and austerity. While these traits can easily be found in Hutten's comic writings, they have too long diverted attention from more positive elements which are also present. The joviality, cheerfulness, and easy enjoyment of humor which are likewise characteristic must be given due consideration, as well. Grimm, Flake, and the others are mistaken, furthermore, in thinking that Hutten's humor can be accurately described in a sentence or two. Such generalization does not do justice to the subject, the diversity of which will be made apparent in the following pages.

We shall return to these critical comments later, when we can better evaluate them further, as we deal with Hutten's handling of the comic. Before doing so, however, we must analyze the *Eov* for their validity as a partial foundation upon which to construct a critique of his humor.

II. THE EPISTOLAE OBSCURORUM VIRORUM

The remarks cited in the Introduction are based for the most part on letters in the *Eov* which have been ascribed to Hutten. Our lack of certainty regarding the true authorship of these letters, however, is one weakness in such appraisals. It is necessary to realize just how little we do know about precisely which satires in the *Eov* Hutten composed. To that end, an examination of the external evidence involved–the statements of Hutten and his contemporaries concerning his contributions–is called for here.

To return to Menius's letter to Crotus Rubeanus, written in 1532, we find there a statement which indicates that Hutten composed at least one letter of the *Eov*. Referring to that work, and, indeed, to *Eov I* specifically, Menius writes: "... which book the famous Erasmus of Rotterdam is said to have doted on so much because of its boundless ridicule of Bishops, Monks, Theologians, etc. that he didn't hesitate to memorize two Letters of that celebrated work, one by you that was the wittiest and most elegant of all and one by Hutten, and to recite them in company."[1]

Hutten corroborates this report in his *Expostulatio cum Erasmo*, written in 1523. Addressing his words to Erasmus, he writes, "When the *Letters of the Obscure* appeared, you more than anyone else praised and applauded them. You all but decreed a triumph for the author. You said that never had a better way been thought of to pursue them [the obscure men] and that this was the best method of barbarously ridiculing the barbarians.

Thus you congratulated us on this success, and when the trifles were not yet printed you copied down some 'to send to my friends in England and France,' you said."[2] The words "you congratulated us" ("gratulabaris ... nobis") imply that Hutten was one of the authors, and, again, the reference is to *Eov I*. Erasmus is said to have written down several of the letters "when the trifles were not yet printed." As soon as the first edition of the *Eov* appeared ("kurz vor dem 19. Oktober 1515," to quote from Bömer[3]), he began to dislike the satires. He would not have sent any of the later letters to his friends.

In his response to Hutten's *Expostulatio*, Erasmus gives us his own account of how he was pleased by some of the early *Eov* and then changed his mind after their publication. In part he states, "I had obtained a copy of one letter about a banquet of magisters that was just a harmless joke and was said to be by Hutten. This gave me the greatest pleasure, and it was read so often among friends that I nearly memorized it."[4] The "banquet of magisters" to which Erasmus alludes indicates that the letter in question is the very first one in the *Eov* as published. It must be the epistle of Thomas Langschneyderius, which is devoted to recounting a banquet attended by some of the obscure men. *Eov II* begins with a similar letter, by one Ioannes Labia, but this piece could hardly be the one in question. It is no doubt of later origin, written in imitation of Langschneyderius's epistle. The latter, then, we are perhaps safe in ascribing to Hutten. Brecht refuses to do so. He assigns all of *Eov I* to Crotus for purely stylistic reasons. On page 26 of his book on the *Eov* he writes, with regard to Erasmus's statement: "Leider hat sich Erasmus ... so unendlich vorsichtig und unbestimmt ausgedrückt, daß man fast nichts daraus ersehen kann. Nur das erfährt man, daß der Brief, der Erasmus im Manuskript zugekommen war und ihm so gut gefiel, daß er ihn fast auswendig konnte, als von Hutten verfaßt galt. Doch war das sicher ein Irrtum; denn der betreffende Brief *de convivio magistrorum, quae nihil haberet praeter innoxium iocum*, I 1, trägt so entschieden und unbezweifelt Crotisches Gepräge, wie nur irgend einer des ersten Teils." Aloys Bömer, on the other hand, accepts Hutten's authorship of the Langschneyderius letter as definite.[5]

It is true that in two letters to Richard Crocus, dated August 9 and August 22, 1516, respectively, Hutten expresses himself in a way which indicates that he at that time knew absolutely nothing about the *Eov*, except that they had been printed and that he was said to be the author. In the earlier letter he asks Crocus to send him a copy, and in the later one he states that the satires have arrived. Regarding rumors to the effect that he himself composed them, he exclaims: "The sophists don't just suspect I'm the author but, as I hear, are openly saying so. Oppose them, stick up for an absent friend, and don't let me be defiled by that dirt."[6] This is grist for Brecht's mill, and the possibility of irony he does not even consider.[7]

Bömer for his part quite correctly views this statement as less than a complete denial.[8]

Admittedly, the evidence that Hutten composed the Langschneyderius letter is not conclusive, but it is the most reliable evidence that we have for his authorship of any of the *Eov* but one. In only one other case can we be as certain that Hutten was the author. That is with *Eov II*, 55.

In a letter to Wilibald Pirckheimer dated April 27, 1517 – some time after the appearance of *Eov II* – Laurenz Behaim says, "And that Hutten, who perchance is the author of the greater part of that book or those epistles, inserted himself, as he writes, defaming himself as though he were a great scoffer or bestial, in order, perhaps, to evade suspicion of being the author."[9] By the phrase "of that book or those epistles" ("illius libelli seu epistolarum") Behaim evidently meant *Eov II* alone, since it was published separately at first, and since the first edition of it probably was the last *Eov* collection to be published before Behaim wrote his letter.[10] If he meant *Eov I* and *II*, he would not have used the genitive singular, "libelli." By his testimony, then, Hutten may have composed most of *Eov II*. Behaim does not assert with positive assurance that Hutten "is the author of the greater part;" he adds the word "forte" – "perchance." Yet we can credit him with the likelihood of being right. Assuming that he is, however, our problems only multiply. Precisely which of the 62 letters in *Eov II* did Hutten write? Behaim himself does not offer much help, but he does indicate that Hutten, by his own testimony ("ut scribit"), wrote about himself, calling himself bestial. Hutten occurs by name in several letters of Part II, namely in numbers 9, 20, 51, 55, and 59. Yet only in *II*, 55, is he called bestial. Magister Sylvester Gricius, writing to Ortvinus Gratius, musters the Reuchlinists and the obscurantists ("qui favent theologis"). Among the former Hutten receives prominent treatment: "... one Ulrich von Hutten, who is very bestial ..." etc.[11]

At the end of the epistle to Erasmus of July 1517 Hutten implies that he is an author of the *Eov*, but he does not specify which of the satires are his;[12] Pirckheimer, in the letter to Hutten of June 26, 1517, is at least as imprecise;[13] and Laurenz Behaim, in another letter to Pirckheimer (this one being dated August 21, 1517), states also that Hutten was an author, but he does not go into any detail. His implication, however, is that Hutten wrote all of *Eov II*, at least: " ... he seems not to deny openly that he published those letters himself ....."[14] But just how the words "those" ("illas") and "published" ("edidisse") are to be understood is not definite.

We take up now a letter from Johann Cochlaeus, written September 9, 1516, to Pirckheimer from Bologna. Cochlaeus relates that Hutten came to dinner and entertained the company by reading some new epistles "multo cum risu." He adds, referring to these same letters: " ... of which one wandered through nearly all of Germany and makes mention of you, because you wrote against usury, which the *magister noster* debated in Bologna."[15] The piece in question can only be *Eov II*, 9, containing Magister Schlauraff's hodoeporicon, lines 39-47 of which agree with what Cochlaeus states was contained in the letter, concerning Pirckheimer. On the matter of Hutten's authorship, Cochlaeus goes on to say: "He denies that he's the author of that work [libelli] by stating, 'not at all; it's God Himself.'" With this evasiveness Hutten created a Gordian knot which has thwarted the sharpest intellects. Brecht and Bömer testify to the unshakable conviction that Hutten is the author, while Paul Merker has made a strong case for his unsung hero, Nikolaus Gerbel. The sad truth of the matter remains, however, that we cannot point with absolute certainty to anyone – Hutten, Gerbel, or another.

On the problem of authorship in general in the *Eov*, Strauß recognizes the difficulties but adds, "Am sichersten scheint mir die Sache bei dem Reisegedicht des M. Schlauraff zu stehen, sofern dieses Hutten in Bologna vorgelesen und die ihm zugemutete Autorschaft mit einem so durchsichtigen Scherzwort abgelehnt hat. Zugleich bildet es ein Seitenstück zu einer ... Elegie in Huttens Querelen, wo ebenso die Muse, wie hier der Dunkelmann, bei sämtlichen dem Dichter bekannten Humanisten Deutschlands die Runde macht."[16] Böcking, in a note to that (tenth) elegy of Hutten's, *In Lossios querelarum liber secundus*, calls attention to Magister Schlauraff's hodoeporicon, saying, "Hutten himself, either intentionally or by chance, distorted this elegy into Schlauraff's 'Carmen rithmicale.'"[17] Yet that is a very bold statement. Brecht accepts it without hesitation,[18] evidently indifferent to the general popularity of the *Reisegedicht* in the Renaissance. The similarity between the two poems is also superficial. In one, Hutten sends his muse on a tour of Germany to visit the poets, while Magister Schlauraff is sent out "habens mandatum a theologis," to incite feeling against Reuchlin. In each poem about fifty humanists are mentioned but only a third of the total are common to each.

Paul Merker, seeing in Magister Schlauraff's letter cogent evidence of the Alsatian Gerbel's authorship, writes that the universities and towns which Gerbel knew are given more attention in the poem than those which Hutten had visited for any length of time, that the German phrases in the poem are in Alsatian, not Franconian, dialect, that Magister Schlauraff encounters a number of humanists connected with printing houses, as Gerbel himself was for much of his life, and that the attention given to Murner would be particularly appropriate coming from Gerbel, who had shortly before moved to Straßburg.[19]

In an article entitled "Verfasser und Drucker der Epistolae obscurorum virorum ..."[20] Bömer succeeds in defending the case for Hutten's authorship of *Eov II*, 9, yet he fails to demolish Merker's case for Gerbel. He argues along with Brecht that Hutten denied having composed *Eov I*, instead of the letters which he read at dinner in Bologna, according to the words used by Cochlaeus: "negat se libelli illius auctorem ...." The new letters are clearly meant, but Hutten was also clearly joking, and he could have been hiding somebody else just as well as himself. If he was not the author, in fact, of *Eov II*, 9, he may not have wanted to state outright that he was not, hoping to get credit for having dealt that particularly telling blow to the obscurantists. Bömer rejects the Alsatian dialect-forms cited by Merker as evidence of Gerbel's authorship, explaining that they occur in Rhenish-Franconian texts and in German writings known to be by Hutten. As for the elegy "Ad poetas Germanos," Bömer agrees with Merker that it constitutes no proof of Hutten's authorship of *Eov II*, 9. He disagrees, however, on the significance of the contents of that satire.

The best evidence for Hutten's having written Magister Schlauraff's letter is that he read it to friends in Bologna. For Bömer that simple fact is evidence enough.[21] Yet we have a letter from Hutten to Gerbel dated July 31, 1516, in which Hutten states that he is sending his friend a new composition, the epistle in verse from Italy (personified) to Emperor Maximilian. Then he adds, "Why don't you do the same for me?"[22] The date of Cochlaeus's letter relating to Pirckheimer the information concerning *Eov II*, 9, is, again, September 9, 1516. The difference in time is just about what we could expect for Gerbel to have received Hutten's letter and to have sent back the *Eov* satires which he had composed. The argument for

Gerbel's authorship of *Eov II*, 9, can be made as convincing as that for Hutten's.

With Cochlaeus's letter we have exhausted all of the external (and hence reliably objective) evidence for Hutten's authorship of particular letters in the *Eov*. We can assume that Hutten wrote many of the letters in *Eov II*, but out of all those in *Eov I* and *II* plus the appendix to *I* we can with any confidence point only to *I*, 1 and *II*, 55 as definitely his work. Two letters out of 110.

How can we refrain from questioning any generalization regarding Hutten's humor which has been predicated largely on the assumption that he composed nearly all, if not all, 62 letters in *Eov II* plus the seven of *Eov I* appendix? Such a judgment may have been determined as much by someone else's work as by Hutten's. Merker cites no fewer than 15 letters in Part II which he says are "wahrscheinlich für Gerbel zu beanspruchen." He also adds, "... wobei ich aber nochmals bemerke, daß es sich bei alledem um provisorische Resultate handelt und die Möglichkeit einer noch größeren Beteiligung des Straßburger Rechtsanwaltes durchaus denkbar, ja mir recht wahrscheinlich ist."[23] He also claims for Gerbel the seven letters in the appendix to *Eov I*.[24] If Gerbel did in fact write *II*, 9, he could have contributed a large number of other epistles, as well.

He is also by no means the only possible author besides Crotus and Hutten. Bömer himself grants Hermann von dem Busche at least four letters in both parts of the *Eov* (*I*, 19 and 36; *II*, 61 and 62) and concedes that Jakob Fuchs, who was with Hutten in Bologna, might have written *II*, 13, 17, 29, and 42.[25] Behaim, in the letter to Pirckheimer of April 27, 1517, says that Fuchs is a possible contributor: "Jakob Fuchs is here [Bamberg] .... He's one of my best friends and an intimate of Ulrich von Hutten. I think he even composed some of the *Letters of Obscure Men*, or at least wasn't far away when some of them were composed."[26] Brecht must have forgotten this statement when he wrote, "Äußere Zeugnisse – daran ist zunächst unbedingt festzuhalten – gibt es für niemanden außer für Crotus und Hutten."[27] Admittedly, Behaim does not assert as a fact the authorship of Jakob Fuchs, but he makes it a possibility with which we have to contend.

In his letter to Reuchlin of January 13, 1517, Hutten implies that many other humanists have joined him in the *Eov*. He writes, "I've been setting a fire that I hope will burst into flame opportunely. ... I'm enlisting those comrades-in-arms who in age and condition are equal to the fray. Soon you'll see the adversaries' mournful tragedy hissed off the stage .... And don't think my comrades in these undertakings are lazy. You'll find each one of them enough for that rabble. Backed by them, I go to the attack."[28] The question arises, of course, as to whether Hutten is referring to *Eov II* with the words "I've been setting a fire" and "Soon you'll see the adversaries' mournful tragedy hissed off the stage." Brecht thinks not. He considers the possibility of more than one author in *Eov II* excluded on stylistic grounds: "Zudem findet sich in Eov II stilistisch gar keine Spur von einer Mitarbeit Vieler."[29] Yet to what could Hutten be better referring than the imminent publication of the second part of the *Eov*? It is not known exactly when these further letters to Ortvinus Gratius appeared. The most that we can say with certainty is that they had been published by the spring of 1517 (see note 10). Hutten wrote the letter to Reuchlin, as was mentioned above, on January 13 of that same year. We are safe in assuming that at that time Part II of the *Eov* was not yet in print. Had it been, Hutten would have pointed to it with satisfaction. Instead, he tells Reuchlin to expect his adversaries soon to be routed. In all probability, he is speaking of *Eov II*.

Whether he means that those "comrades-in-arms" whom he has recruited were themselves participants in the writing of the *Eov* is not more certain. Perhaps they were, however, and again we must reckon with the possibility. This possibility is supported by statements in Menius's letter to Crotus Rubeanus. Paragraph 23 reads in part: "I'm leaving out many other Poets, some of them learned, whom you roused with the occult Epistles [occultis ... Epistolis] and summoned to make fun of the puppets of the Roman Church...."[30] Brecht argues that with the expression "occultis ... Epistolis" Menius did mot mean the *Eov* (*Eov I*) but rather some secret letters which Crotus supposedly sent around to his friends: "Es handelt sich ... ganz allgemein um geheime Briefe, in denen Crotus andere Humanisten zur satirischen Schriftstellerei gegen Rom aufgereizt hat ...."[31] This interpretation strikes one immediately as far-fetched, and it is weakened by another sentence from Menius's letter, relating substantially what is contained in the quotation above but making somewhat clearer what Menius had in mind. This sentence reads, partly, "... not to mention that book of yours which could keep ten Democrituses busy, namely the *Letters of Obscure Men*, which were nothing if not a trumpet for summoning and arming against the papists with new invective those who by themselves would not have invented such witty sayings."[32] Here there can be no doubt that the *Eov* are meant – no "geheime Briefe." Furthermore, it appears that the new works through which the papists are attacked must be the letters of *Eov II*. The clear implication is that these new works were written in the manner of the original *Dunkelmännerbriefe*. We cannot be absolutely sure that Menius is reminding Crotus of how he stirred a number of humanists to imitate his work in *Eov II*, yet this interpretation of Menius's words seems justified and cannot be disproved. Not only may Hermann von dem Busche and Jakob Fuchs have participated in that collection; other writers may have, as well.

Brecht insists that the style of *Eov II*, as of *Eov I*, is uniform, and that the style of *Eov I* appendix agrees with that of *Eov II*. Only Hutten can have composed the appendix to *I* and all of *II*.[33] Yet how reliable can stylistic analysis be with the *Eov*? Richard Newald explains its limitations in such a work by saying, "Es ist immer schwer, aus inhaltlichen und stilistischen Kriterien eine solche Gemeinschaftsarbeit ihren Urhebern richtig zuzuteilen. Gerade bei satirischen Werken, zu denen mehrere Verfasser Material, Gedanken und Einfälle zusammentragen, der einzelne seine Beiträge liefert, die der Letzte redigiert, wird sich nie der fröhliche Zechgenosse feststellen lassen, welcher zu dem Werk einen Zug oder Gedanken bei einem Symposion beigesteuert hat."[34] We should not stop with a mere "Zug oder Gedanke"; in the *Eov* whole letters are just as questionable. Bömer, who, as we have seen, admits Busch and Fuchs as likely contributors along with Hutten and Crotus (though on a much smaller scale), adds this thought: "Aber auch die ganze Komposition der Briefe ist doch nicht derart, weder bei Eov I, noch bei Eov II, daß nicht auch einmal einem andern, wenn er ein paar Muster vor sich hatte – und wir haben gehört, daß manche Briefe schon einzeln im Freundeskreise die Runde machten –, ein solches kleines Stück gelungen sein sollte."[35] In spite of this statement, though, Bömer modifies Brecht's thesis only slightly.

Two comments by Laurenz Behaim in letters to Pirckheimer show that among the German humanists imitating the *Eov* style may have been something of a fad. In the earlier letter, the one from August 21, 1517, Behaim, having shown Hutten some writings of which Hutten disapproved, gives vent to his feelings by saying, "But I think he doesn't want it [the material] published because he sees that others have the same ability or style that he used in the *Letters of the Obscure* ...."[36] It is true that this sentence also indicates Hutten to have been jealous and not likely to have admitted other contributors to the *Eov*, of which he seems to have taken control after the publication of Part I. Yet on the basis of this single remark by Behaim, which is only conjectural in the first place, it would be going too far to argue that Hutten alone must have written *Eov II*. In the other letter, dated February 9, 1518, Behaim relates that Fabius Zonarius wrote a number of works against Ortvinus Gratius, Arnold von Tungern, and the Cologne inquisitor Hochstraten. These works, moreover, Zonarius composed "in the manner and style of the obscure men."[37] This statement by Behaim is certainly not evidence that Zonarius is to be considered an author of the *Eov*. The date February 9, 1518, falls after the publication of even the second edition of *Eov II*. Zonarius could have had something included in *Eov II* which Behaim is not sending to Pirckheimer, but to assume so would be unwarranted. The point here is only that since Zonarius did imitate the *Eov*, others may have done so too. Certainly, in any case, the style is not difficult to copy, and stylistic analysis cannot be depended upon for conclusive proof.

Before we leave the *Eov*, it is necessary to make clear that we do have reason to consider Hutten the author of much of Part II. We can, with the likelihood of being right, assign a large number of specific letters to him besides *I*, 1 and *II*, 55. All 29 letters in *Eov I* appendix and *Eov II* which are dated from Rome could well be from Hutten, although Bömer exaggerates in saying of them, "Der größte Teil ... verrät so starke Lokalkenntnis, daß er nur von jemand geschrieben sein kann, der wirklich mit den römischen bezw. italienischen Verhältnissen aus eigener Anschauung genau vertraut war, wie das bei Hutten zutrifft."[38] Hutten can easily have communicated to other humanists not in Rome at the time certain details of Roman conditions, such as the heat of the summer of 1516. In regard to the seventh letter of the appendix to Part I, where Hochstraten (who supposedly wrote the epistle) laments the sad state of his affairs in Rome, Merker shows that it conforms essentially to the close of Hutten's letter to Gerbel of July 31, 1516, sent from Bologna: "Es liegt sonach die Vermutung nicht fern, daß Gerbelius nach Empfang dieses echten Huttenbriefes ... die darin stehenden Mitteilungen aus Italien mit seiner starken Phantasie ausmalte und sich in die fatale Situation Hochstratens versetzte: das Resultat war der das Datum des 22. August tragende letzte Anhangsbrief."[39]

Whereas Bömer notes, also as evidence of Hutten's authorship, that some details from Bologna occur toward the close of *Eov II* (and Hutten was in Bologna after leaving Rome), they are not conclusive proof, though they do point principally to him. We should remember that Hutten wrote at least the one letter to Gerbel from Bologna. The other details from *Eov II* which Bömer lists as having counterparts in Hutten's known works and personal experiences also do not constitute definitive proof.[40]

The point of this critique of *Eov* scholarship is not to deny Hutten a significant role in the composition of the *Dunkelmännerbriefe* but rather to insist on caution. Despite the fact that Bömer's conclusions appear to have won general acceptance today, they are far less impregnable than Bömer himself indicates them to be. His scholarship is keen, and, building on the foundation laid by Brecht, he has done probably as much as can be to clarify the manifold obscurities of the *Verfasserproblem*. Nevertheless, we must reconcile ourselves to the hard truth that we cannot know with absolute certainty just who the authors of this satirical classic were and just which letters each wrote. Any attempt to hide the unresolvable questions behind categorical assertions (a common practice in *Eov* scholarship) only compounds the difficulties.

The lack of certainty as to which letters Hutten wrote makes the *Eov* treacherous grounds for the support of any judgment on his humor and forces us to omit these satires from further consideration.

III. HUTTEN'S USE AND APPRECIATION OF JOCULARITY

One of the most interesting aspects of Hutten's humor is his occasional use of joking remarks. It is an aspect regularly neglected by students of his works. Those who share Fife's view of the supposedly characteristic austerity should acknowledge that it is offset now and then by jocosity. Hutten also remarks several times about sharing jokes with his friends. Indeed, at least at one point in his far from easy life he felt the need for having a jovial wife with whom he could share the laughter of a lighter moment. It is true that his jocular humor is unobtrusive in comparison to the satire, and if the reader is not on the lookout for it, it may make no particular impression on him. A certain amount of joking is nevertheless to be found, and it must be accorded due consideration.

To discover the "true Hutten," Hutten as his acquaintances knew him, we can do no better today than to turn to his correspondence. We do so knowing full well that many of his letters he wrote for publication and that he may have been striking a pose when he seems most natural. Still, there should be on the whole less danger of artificiality in his correspondence than in his other works. To learn, then, what laughter meant to him personally, in his day-to-day affairs, we read his letters with particular attention.

Fife makes a curious comment on them in his article cited in the initial pages of this study. Speaking of austerity still, he goes on to say:

There is more than a suggestion of this in his

HUTTEN'S USE AND APPRECIATION OF JOCULARITY

> letters, so far as we have them. They show a direct and dynamic spirit: enthusiasm for "good letters," passion for reform in education and religious usages, sincerity in friendship, bitter hatred of public and private enemies; but we look in vain for any melting into real intimacy. This is not because they are almost all in Latin... Whatever the cause: inhibitions of caste, persistent self-consciousness, or an inborn dread of self-analysis, we feel a kind of spiritual self-withdrawal in Hutten even in the most personal self-delineation, like the famous letter to Pirckheimer of 1518....[1]

Fife's implication is that Hutten was normally cold and impersonal. Although he is so in many of his letters, he is not in all of them. A number of times he erupts with enthusiasm for someone whom he admires—Sickingen, for instance, or Erasmus, or Albrecht von Mainz. Letters from other humanists to friends who knew Hutten show him to have been out-going and affable, if also irascible and outspoken. He was a socializer and an organizer, as we have seen in regard to the *Eov*. He liked people and was always eager to make new acquaintances. The reason that his letters contain little about his feelings is that he was not an introspective person by nature. Through all of his hardship that circumstance no doubt proved a blessing.

Few people have lived a life of greater physical suffering. Hutten was in pain through nearly all of his productive years. His body ran at times with sores. In his fascinating and historically significant book on the disease that finally killed him after some fifteen years of torment, he gives a horrendously graphic description of his physical corrosion. At one point a friend went so far as to advise suicide, he tells us there.² In view of his suffering, hence, the frequent cheerfulness which his letters radiate is a source of continual amazement. It is true that with his last frustration, disappointment, and failure, bitterness wins out. Facetiousness does not brighten his final writings, but that we find it anywhere is, under the circumstances, a matter of some importance.

Of particular significance is the fact that he could joke about his very pain. For eight years he limped from a bony protuberance above his left ankle.³ He tells us in an epigram that his foot hurt so badly at the siege of Pavia in 1513 that he would have been content to die.⁴ Yet in a letter to Balthasar Fachus from the previous year he refers to his miserable condition by saying, "I'm still imitating Vulcan...."⁵

Nor was he so austere that he could not laugh at his own compositions. In the letter to Eitelwolf vom Stein written as the preface to the panegyric *In laudem Alberti Archiepiscopi Moguntini* Hutten facetiously explains that he wrote the work in order to induce others to take pen in hand. He will succeed, he adds, "... for who, when he has seen these, won't want at once to write better things?"⁶ In the letter to Bonifatius Amerbach of October 26, 1519, he makes a similar remark in saying, "Because you write that you have my little works in your hands every day I don't know if it isn't to be feared you're neglecting better ones."[7]

In marked contrast to their later internecine strife is the early praise exchanged between Hutten and the greatest wit and intellect of the age, Erasmus. Worthy of the latter is this jokingly exaggerated compliment: "You made Gregor Coppus, the other doctor of the prince [Albrecht von Mainz], completely Erasmian. He always has your labors in his hands, and hardly anyone else reads them as avidly. For this reason many people are angry with you. They say you're making Theologians out of Medics."[8]

Contradicting Hutten's supposed austerity is his frequent indulgence in word-play. Böcking, in regard to the line from an epigram, "Italia's mobile; noble she was before," comments, "This kind of word-play [mobilis–nobilis] is rare in Hutten's writings, cold as he is."[9] As an indication that word-play is not so uncommon in his works, however, a few examples may be cited. Of the reformer Oecolampadius Hutten writes in the long letter to Pirckheimer of 1518, "Coming from Basel yesterday, Oecolampadius, whom I hadn't seen before, approached me. He's a toothed theologian whose teeth, avidly chewing the Scriptures in three languages, those toothless ones envy."[10] The compliment may strike the reader as grotesque, but it is, perhaps for that very reason, effective. On the same page Hutten continues, after lauding Erasmus and Guillaume Budé, "adde Fabrum

[Lefèvre d'Étaples], qui philosophiam exquisite fabrefecit illustrato Aristotele." In the letter to Eoban Hessus and Peter Eberbach dated August 3, 1519, where Hutten complains of being neglected by his friends, he inquires particularly about Mutianus Rufus. In part he says, "Send greetings from me respectfully and, lest Mutian be mute, admonish him."[11]

If we peruse the principal works, the dialogues, we find word-plays there as well, though not always free of inanity. In *Febris prima* Fever has importuned Hutten to recommend a host for her since he refuses to receive her himself. He finally comes up with the right person, a *Curtisan* who learned the sweet life at a Roman cardinal's. "Quodsi me non accipiat ille," asks the insatiable Fever, "tunc tu quo duces?" "Circumducam," replies Hutten. She in turn quips, "At te ego circumscribam," etc.[12]

Siegfried Szamatolski shows that Hutten used some ingenuity in translating word-plays from Latin into German with the dialogue *Vadiscus*: "Hutten hat in seiner Übersetzung keine lateinischen Wortspiele, wenngleich sie die Vorlage bietet und wenngleich mehrere neu geschaffene deutsche Wortspiele seine Neigung bezeugen, auch die Übersetzung mit Wortspielen zu zieren: *superstitione ... religionem*: 'aberglaubens ... rechten glauben' ... *sine religione* 'vnangesehen was geboten oder verbotten ist' ... So lässt er das Wortspiel *pretio prece* ... fallen. Geschickt gibt er wieder *discordem concordiam* 'zwiträchtigen eintracht' ... mit bewunderungswürdiger Geschicklichkeit *concilium* ... *conciliabulum* 'rat ... rott' ...."[13]

The dialogue *Bulla*, which is particularly rich in word-play, is actually constructed upon a pun. The word *bulla* itself has the double meaning "bull" and "bubble." Hutten treats the title figure (the caricatured *Exurge domine* which appears in Germany and attacks Liberty, to whose rescue the valiant knight betakes himself) as nothing more than a bubble, one filled, however, not with air but with corruption. After haranguing her abusively (partly with insulting word-play such as *bulga* and *ampulla*), Hutten pounds the vainglorious virago until she bursts.[14]

The work *Nemo* is also based on word-play, insofar as "Nobody" is treated as somebody. In the preface Hutten toys with this ambiguity. Addressing his old friend, he writes: "Then accept this Nothing, Crotus, which you bewailed has been written by me for a whole year – repeating that twenty times in your letter with, as it were, tragic lament – as though something could be extorted from somebody who is nothing. Now I send you this Nothing and in such a way that Nobody brings it. With whom does Nothing more rightly consort than Nobody, since nobody writes and does nothing?" etc.[15]

Hutten, it should be added here, not only jokes with words in this preface; he also jokes with himself. He calls himself Nemo.[16] He tells Crotus that he was treated like a nobody on his (first) return from Italy. Quoting a line from the poem,

he states, "Behold that Nobody who says of himself
'Nobody gives good studies their due rewards.'"[17] By calling himself a nobody, Hutten invites the reader to laugh at him, albeit sympathetically. As we shall see subsequently, he used his own person comically in a number of cases, a point which further belies his supposed austerity and coldness.

If these examples serve to qualify the belief that Hutten was stern and severe, by indicating that he liked to use words and ideas jokingly, as well as satirically, then the following remarks should indicate further that his humor was not merely the handmaiden of anger. These statements by Hutten testify to his enjoyment of the humor of others and to his own habit of sharing anecdotes.

The first are from the letter to Jakob Fuchs lamenting the death of the friend and patron Eitelwolf vom Stein. Here Hutten relates several of the witticisms of Stein which made a particular impression on him. He writes that Stein was not "an inept wit, even *ex tempore*," and, among others, these examples follow: When the Venetian war was said to have been written of most elegantly, Stein moaned, "If only it had been fought as well!" And when some fellow with scarred visage boasted that he had stood in the face of the enemy, Stein put him down by observing, "And he in yours, I see."[18]

According to his own testimony Hutten laughed more often than his writings on the whole might lead one to believe. In the letter to Konrad Peutinger from Mainz, May 25, 1518, he tells a little about his life at court. He mentions his special friend Heinrich Stromer, the archbishop's physician: "He's forthright, dextrous, and open. He hates pretense, despises pomp, and often teaches me adages. I tell him in turn my jokes, since I saw that he's that way."[19] In the letter to Pirckheimer of October 25, 1518, Hutten informs us that Georg von Streitberg visited him often during the Guaiac cure and entertained him with an exchange of anecdotes: "... for often he sat for hours mixing funny stories with me ..."[20] Not only did Hutten enjoy making fun of his fellow men; he liked also to laugh *with* his friends. Marquardus Fotzenhut seems to have been justified in calling him one "qui semper ridet."[21]

Hutten explains to Pirckheimer, furthermore, in the letter just mentioned that if he took the advice which the Nürnberger had sent him he would have no anecdotes with which to amuse himself and those around him. Pirckheimer had criticized Hutten's dialogue *Aula* as childish and advised the author to leave court and retire to quiet in the company of the muses.[22] Hutten replies, not at all offended, in a tone too serious not to bespeak sincerity: "If I obliged you and buried myself completely in that scholastic quietude, giving myself up to studies and applying my mind to the writing of books – for which I don't know how I seem to you to be suited – what would I have that I could pleasantly share with my companions in study when we want to relax? Not experiencing anything, what stories would I have to contribute?"[23]

He wanted amusing anecdotes to share, and by the spring of 1519 Hutten had begun to speak of wanting a wife to share them with. He was 31 years old and, though not at all interested in a life of inactivity, still ready to settle down with a family (something which might have saved him from the folly of the *Pfaffenkrieg*). In May of that year he wrote to Friedrich Fischer, asking his friend to help find the proper girl. In this letter he describes what he wants, and among the traits which his wife is to have are cheerfulness, he says, and a sense of humor: "I need someone to have fun with when I relax from cares and even from my more acrid studies – someone to play and joke with, to share pleasant and light anecdotes with.... Get me a wife, Friedrich, and in order that you know what kind, get an attractive one, rather young, well educated, cheerful, modest, patient...."[24]

In the letter to Arnold von Glauburg, where he writes apprehensively about the prospect Kunigunde, whose mother seems to have viewed him with reservations, Hutten cites as one of his own attractions his joking disposition: "There's nothing I'd rather know than how her mother is disposed .... And as far as her [the mother's] temper is concerned, which is said to be easily provokable, I hope more and more when she gets to know my ways and sees her girl loved by me dearly and herself treated with respect and that all of you get along with me on the best of terms and that

HUTTEN'S USE AND APPRECIATION OF JOCULARITY

there's nothing wild, nothing troublesome in me, that even my studies are full of pleasantry, jokes, and wit, she'll bear me and let herself be borne."[25]

Hutten's statements about his use and appreciation of jocularity do not agree with the judgment of his biographers and critics. A discrepancy between what they have affirmed and what he reveals becomes easily apparent apart from his satire. In the following pages we will see that some of his satire also constitutes an exception to the prevailing opinion of his humor.

IV. HUTTEN'S IRONIC SATIRE

Most of Hutten's humor is satiric. This fact probably goes a long way to explain why his humor in general has been thought of as acrid and unappealing. It is a mistake, however, to assume that all satire, or all of Hutten's satire, is severe. Some of Hutten's ridicule is quite good-natured, and there are times, as we have already begun to see, when it is even directed at himself – hardly characteristic of a grim and dour disposition.

By far his favorite satiric tool was caricature (which will be considered in the following section), but he did use some irony, as well. To him, as to other Renaissance writers – and, in fact, to some writers today – sheer invective, unembellished with any comic elements, was also satire. Satire evidently meant to him any kind of literary attack. A diatribe against Pope Julius II he entitled *In tempora Iulii satyra*,[1] even though there is nothing whatsoever amusing about the piece. Since we are concerned only with his use of the comic, however, the great amount of such straight invective in his writings warrants no attention here. Although Hutten on at least this one occasion labeled simple abuse as "satire," we cannot infer that he considered it humorous. If someone could show that he did, we would indeed have cause to consider his sense of humor odd, as Fife implies it was; but evidence to prove this notion seems wanting.

Quite in keeping with the previous pronouncements on his humor, however, is the crude irony of sarcasm in which Hutten occasionally indulged.

HUTTEN'S IRONIC SATIRE

In the collection of epigrams *De statu Romano* we read, for example:

> Come, gentlemen, join in and live by plundering;
> Be wicked men who desecrate and kill.
> Come, mix the sacred and profane, get used to pomp,
> And run the gamut of debauchery.
> Feel free to speak your mind and do the worst you've said;
> Of course you won't believe in any gods.
> We saw all this in Rome (what's holier than she?)
> With heaven's gates as open as before.
> Just carry gold to Rome, and virtue will be yours;
> Whoever doesn't know it's bought is mad.
> If vice is what you want, Rome markets it as well;
> So once again I'll tell you, men, be wicked![2]

In the fourth oration against the duke of Württemberg, referring to his murdered cousin Hans, Hutten might have written the following in gall, so bitter is it: "... as the wounds show, you attacked from behind, without warning, as everyone believes. And you want to be known as an outstanding warrior and magnanimous Swabian prince. As if you had killed several thousand of the enemy, you'll ask perhaps for a triumphal procession ...."[3] In the same speech (p. 77) this sentence reminds one of the dialogue *Phalarismus*: "Behold the impudence of the man: I believe he would have us commend him for not killing Ludwig, too, who was waiting at court for his brother, and for not slaying Agapetus Hutten with him. He says he didn't murder all our kinfolk there as he could have and will boast that by his generosity they're still alive."

The same spirit moves in some of the glosses to the bull *Exurge domine*. The sarcasm is rather puerile, as when the pope speaks of how he could treat Luther but decides, " ... nevertheless, on the advice of our brothers and imitating the clemency of God Almighty, who does not desire the death of the sinner but rather that he be converted and live, having forgotten all of the injuries inflicted hitherto on us and on the Apostolic Chair, we decided to use all possible piety ..." and Hutten responds, "Oh clemency incredible! No one thought Leo could be so merciful, especially when he could kill."[4] In another instance he befouls the perfumed sanctity of Leo ("Moreover we warn all ... the faithful ... to avoid the heretics ... after the above-mentioned deadline has passed ... and to minister to them in no way") by gibing, "Not even to hold the chamber pot?" (pp. 327-328). At the end, when Leo says that the heretics can be expected to take cognizance of the bull, "since it is not likely that things so clear should remain unknown to them," Hutten retorts, "To help out in this difficulty we have undertaken to republish it. It is very important to us that such a splendid bull be circulated as widely as possible" (p. 330).

Putting his sarcasm aside, let us consider now

some other ways in which Hutten uses irony. At the opening of the dialogue *Inspicientes* we discover an instance of what is called "cosmic irony." In contrast to sarcasm, which belittles bitterly by means of an ostensibly positive remark, such as any of the foregoing, cosmic irony shows how inherently small many things actually are by measuring them on the almost infinite scale of relativity. Our own daily routine, for instance, may seem very important to us, but if we compare our activities to the movements of planets and stars, they will (let us hope) appear somewhat less momentous. To Sol and Phaethon of *Inspicientes*, as they traverse the earth high in their chariot, the grand undertakings of men dwindle to something like the officiousness of insects. Phaethon remarks, "It's been a long time since we observed sublunary doings as we used to. We've covered ourselves by a large mass of clouds so we couldn't see men running around here, some sailing about there, and others fighting among themselves and leading out great armies over trifles, dying for an empty name and some titles snatched through ambition."[5] This ironic tone is not maintained, however. *Inspicientes* quickly becomes a non-satiric lesson in German customs, changing at the end into the caricature of Cajetan, to which we will give some attention in the following section.

Gottfried Niemann finds Socratic method in the questions of Misaulus in *Aula* and of Sickingen in *Praedones*.[6] This is evidence, he says, of influence on Hutten from Plato's dialogues. While Misaulus and Sickingen do not feign ignorance, Fortuna, in the work bearing her name, may be employing Socratic irony in the discussion of Providence. She seems to try to lead Hutten with her queries toward a recognition of the relationship of chance to Providence.[7] At first she appears to know nothing about the matter. When Hutten asks whether Providence exists, she says, very evasively, "Some think so. I do know that I exist." Further, "I likewise know that Jove exists, who blinded me. That Providence you inquire about, however, is refuted by the success of wicked men" (p. 83). She causes Hutten to argue in behalf of Providence himself until he finds a satisfactory way to reconcile it with evil and misfortune in the world. "But look, you!" he finally exclaims, "I've got a solution now to the whole problem: God doesn't reward good works or punish men for their evil deeds here. He reserves His judgment for the eternal kingdom and future life" (p. 86). When Fortuna attempts to go a step further and asks, "Why don't you attribute what happens here to chance, reserving those future matters for God," Hutten fearfully avoids the question by replying, "Because religion doesn't teach this." He shies away from the ultimate conclusion on this occasion, though on others he appears not to have done so.[8] By means of Socratic irony, as it seems, Fortuna leads Hutten on, if without complete success. Insofar as he is blind to his intellectual inferiority, he is laughable.

In the preface to *Aula* he feigns anger at his friend Stromer because of the peril which he has supposedly incurred by writing the dialogue and blames Stromer for persuading him to undertake a project with such potentially dire consequences. In the process he makes fun of himself again: "Already my head, my face, my jaws are shaking, and I seem to see one of the courtly giants draw back a six-pound fist to plant against my cheek. If that happens, I'm afraid you'll laugh up your sleeve and think it's sport to have me slapped, my face smashed up, my teeth knocked out" etc.[9] In that letter to Pirckheimer of October 25, 1518, Hutten theatrically bewails the fate of *Nemo*: "[Oecolampadius] said that Erasmus has gone back to his Brabant folk and that my *Nemo* is being printed again by Froben. Oh those perversely officious chalcographers, that impetuous breed! Now my trifles will wander through France and be thrown to those ulcerous theologians who're offended whenever they're touched. There won't be much hope for Hutten. Woe is me! I'm finished, done for!" etc.[10]

Nemo itself is an early instance of Hutten's irony. It is, as a matter of fact, the very earliest instance of his use of the comic which we have.[11] Here the humor derives from nothing more than personification of the abstract "nobody," as in the sentence "Nobody can serve two masters." Hutten varies this idea through a number of verses then expands it in the description of a house where, in the absence of their master, the servants have wreaked total chaos. When the master returns, "Nobody" takes the blame. The joke is appallingly simple, if also well done, and we might concur in the evident sneer of Erasmus: "Hutten amused himself with a book, the title of which is *Nobody*. Nobody is unaware that the subject matter is ridiculous...."[12] For the student of Hutten's humor, however, the work, especially the earlier version, is important precisely because of its simple merriment.

Heinrich Grimm's comment, "Tiefster Ernst steht hinter seinem [Hutten's] Lachen," (p. 4 of this study) was made in connection with *Nemo*. It may well have been this statement that prompted Fife to write, "A certain austerity can be noted in Hutten, even in *Nemo*, where he bases on a literary tradition of folklike humor" (p. 2). Grimm's remark is not appropriate for *Nemo*, however, and is contradicted in the sentence which follows it, where we read: "Bewußt wollte Hutten mit dem Nemo einen heiteren Wechsel in die Strenge des Alltags bringen, düstere Tage durch fröhliche Stunden erfreuen, die munteren Scherze sollten nicht mit gerunzelter Stirn aufgenommen werden."[13]

The last phrase is one which Hutten uses. In the introductory lines to the later as well as the earlier version he has Nemo inform the reader that what follows is to be read after all seriousness has been put aside: "Don't read these facile jokes with rigid brow." One should not always be in earnest, Nemo says; laughter has its place.[14] Hutten evidently knew as well as Erasmus that this little piece of verse is ridiculous, and he felt it advisable to put his readers at the outset in a jocular frame of mind.

It has been said of *Nemo* that it shows Hutten to have passed through a period of skepticism, since the theme of the composition is supposed to be "Alles ist nichts und Niemand ist etwas."[15] Although the skepticism has been over-emphasized, *Nemo* does have some rather pessimistically satiric lines, particularly in the later version. A few examples are:

>Nobody lives contentedly with what he has.
>   Nobody learns to tolerate his lot.

or

>Nobody's good, and Nobody's wholly satisfied.

or

>Nobody gets ahead with innocence. At court
>   Nobody honest seeks important posts.[16]

Nemo I shows this worldly cynicism to a much smaller degree. Originally Hutten seems to have had virtually no satiric intent when he blended together two already-existing treatments of the *Nemo-Stoff*.[17] With the 1510 version he was simply retelling some old jokes. By strengthening the skeptical element in the later version, he created stronger satire but a kind of satire that was not typical of him.[18] *Nemo II* is not angry and vindictive, and its satire is rather cynical. Generally Hutten's satire is very positive and fired with reformatory fervor, as the previous remarks on his humor indicate. Paul Held, who stresses the skeptical element of *Nemo II*, also observes that the frame of mind which produced it was not of long duration and that this type of satire is exceptional for Hutten.[19]

The added cynicism in the later version does not keep the work from still being basically a "poetic joke," to borrow Strauß's term.[20] Although the total length was increased from 96 to 156 verses, roughly one-third of the increase falls within the second, narrative part, which is satiric only in making fun of our foible of putting the blame for something on somebody else. Of the lines added to the epigrammatic part of the work, about one-third are merely playful, as "Nobody's greater than the German Emperor" (p. 113).

Grimm makes a statement in regard to the 1518 version which implies that it was received as a daring attack on the *status quo*. He says, "Was bisher keiner sich politisch zu sagen getraut hatte, war durch Hutten in der Nemo-Einkleidung gesagt worden. Gewisse Kreise sahen in Nemo den leibhaftigen Teufel, die Nemopersonifikation wurde im literarischen Kampf gefürchtet." Grimm does not support this claim with any creditable evidence, however. All the documentation that he gives for Nemo's supposedly having been thought "the devil himself" is the note that somebody has written the one word *Diabole* on the copy of the work in the Munich library. In support of the idea that Nemo was feared "im literarischen Kampf" Grimm merely cites the verses from the

HUTTEN'S IRONIC SATIRE

title page of Hutten's *Beklagunge der Freistette deutscher nation:*

> Der Nemo hatt das gedicht gemacht
> Das mancher jm regiment nit lacht
> Er sey königk bischoff fuerst oder graff
> Den allen die ungerechtigkeit leufft nach.[21]

From the sportive pessimism of *Nemo* we go now to the more vigorous irony of the Fever-dialogues. Here we are in the realm of Hutten's standard satire. Of the two colloquies, the earlier, *Febris I*, is the more unified and also the more successful as humor. Its comic effect results from the fact that Fever wants to dwell among voluptuaries, so Hutten recommends various of the clergy on the basis of their dissolute living. Qualities which are in reality negative become positive for his purposes. In paragraph 11, for instance, Hutten suggests, "And because you say you're to deal with sybarites, follow me. We'll go to those brothers who always have an easy time of it, since they're fat and sleek, and who live pleasantly and sweetly and stay in their cells so they rarely get the exercise that's bad for you. They also drink wine and are very intemperate about eating fish. Here's worthy lodging."[22] Hutten has great latitude in this work to paint ecclesiastic corruption in lurid colors. Almost everything that he might say would remain within the pale of humor. He never grows violent, however, nor does he misuse this opportunity of insulting the clergy in the name of humor by prolonging his descriptions of, to Fever, "recommendable" attributes. *Febris I* is short. The author seems to have had a good idea here of what constitutes a just mean. After rejecting Cajetan, artisans, princes, rich men, merchants and the Fuggers, monks, and canons in general, Fever settles for that *Curtisan* "who returned recently from Rome, where he had learned the sweet life at some cardinal's, threw himself at once into the midst of delights, and is living quite enjoyably" (p. 37). His qualifications are exellent, and Hutten is exuberant in "praise" of him.

In the sequel Fever returns. Here the irony stems from her avowed pity for clerics beset by concubines. In telling Hutten how mistresses misuse the clergy, she purports to be lamenting the misery of the latter when in fact she is describing their decadence. "Apart from the fact that those with concubines ruin the more noble part of themselves, their soul, they have to spend lavishly on food and clothes to please those girl friends, and they wear themselves out with their profligacy," she says. "Each one also casts away his character for love of them." Hutten asks, "Then those who keep concubines sacrifice everything?" "If they're devoted, I don't see why not," Fever replies. Hutten is moved. "You'll soon have *me* saying they're pitiful," he confesses, and Fever exclaims, "Saying they are! Is anyone more pitiful than they, living as they do, with all their expenses, never having peace of mind, never having anyone reliable around them?"[23] This "compassion" is vitiated, however, by not being the only reason why Fever returns. Other diseases were crowding her out, and she says, of all things, that Jupiter commanded her to come back! Both of these points we find expressed when Hutten remarks, "... I take it that as long as priests have concubines you won't have anything more to do with them," and Fever replies, "Nothing, since Jupiter forbids me to and since they have enough diseases already" (p. 130). The irony, furthermore, is not sustained to the end but yields eventually to direct censure.

The comments that have been made hitherto on Hutten's humor in general apply to *Febris II*. They reflect the notion that with him always the comic tends to pale before sternness and anger. This last dialogue, where indignation becomes too impatient of restraint to follow through with even the pretense of a humorous treatment of the subject, can be considered a case in point, along with most of the incidental sarcasm scattered through Hutten's writings. With *Febris I*, where "tiefster Ernst steht hinter seinem Lachen" also, the ironic method is not abandoned once it has been adopted, so that while grimness is apparent, it is not detrimental. *Nemo* is a major case of non-conformity to the broad statements on Hutten's humor, except insofar as its skepticism might be considered austere. At least *Nemo*, like some of the minor instances of irony that we have seen, was not born of anger. The following section should further show that generalizations on Hutten's humor have not taken adequately into account even the scope of his varied satire.

V. HUTTEN'S USE OF CARICATURE

Having sampled Hutten's irony, we are now to give some attention to his principal type of satire, caricature. The material that we will examine in this section is divided into two groups. The first and larger is caricature of others; the second, of the author himself.

Taking the first group, let us consider two examples of Hutten's epigrams caricaturing the nations and people involved in the wars in Italy during his first sojourn there, 1512-1513. In one of these he ridicules, though not without qualification, his own homeland for the national vice of overindulgence in alcohol, while also taking France and Venice to task for failings which are exaggerated to the point of being, along with the German fondness for wine, identifying characteristics:

> Venetians, French, and Germans covet Latium;
>   Deceitful one, one proud, one steeped in wine –
> All odious. "Apollo, grant the lightest yoke,"
>   Prays Italy, and Phoebus says, "The French
> Are always proud; Venetians, always full of guile;
>   The Germans, though, not always drunk –
> choose one!"[1]

In a number of these epigrams the caricature is more obvious, insofar as France is portrayed as a cock (*gallus*) and Venice, as a toad in the manner of *Marcus*, but in any case the satire is rather crude and tends to justify the common opinion on Hutten's sense of humor. More amusing, perhaps, is this light travesty of the Venetian commander Bartolomeo d'Alviano:

44

> If good the fight, you swear; if not so good, you swear.
> At rest you do the same, Bartholomew.
> In victory you swear; you swear when slipping up.
> In camp you swear, at market, and at court.
> You swear when you're in service, swear when banqueting;
> You swear shipwrecked upon the open sea.
> In arms you swear; you swear togated and at peace.
> You swear with jokes as well as earnest things.
> By day you swear, and night brings shadows while you swear,
> As Cynthia is borne by dusky steeds.
> Since everywhere you swear, by swearing tell me this:
> What don't you do, Bartholomew, by swearing?[2]

Here we find Hutten surprisingly playful. If he wrote this burlesque in anger, there is at any rate no viciousness apparent. In it we have a piece of satire less typical of him than the longer caricatures on the Venetians, *Marcus* and *De piscatura Venetorum*.

The title *Marcus*, while taken from the patron saint of Venice, is in Hutten's lampoon the name given to a megalomaniacal toad that is evidently the embodiment of Venetian spirit. It emerges from the Adriatic swollen with proud ambition and pulls on a lion's pelt. After summoning the people of the region, the toad proclaims that the Fate of Rome ("Sors Romana") has appeared to it, declaring that the Empire of the Caesars will be transferred to its power. Therewith the Venetians crown the toad King Marcus and embark on wars of conquest. All the world defers to them, except Germany. When Marcus attempts to reach the heavens, Jupiter dispatches the German eagle to humble the upstart. Such is this modest heroicomic beast epic. Its full title, it might be added, reveals an ironic touch: *Marcus heroicum*. Böcking notes in regard to the *De piscatura Venetorum heroicum* that Hutten was being satiric in calling these works "heroics."[3] They definitely are written in heroic verse, yet we may assume that the author was artful enough to want his form, and consequently his title, to add a touch of the ludicrous. If he had not overworked his *Marcus* idea in the epigrams, we might enjoy its humor more.[4]

The *De piscatura Venetorum* is similar to *Marcus* in subject matter but inferior as satire. Here the Venetians are caricatured as poor fishermen, who, joined by the scum of the earth, gradually grow in wealth until they have the power to conquer. Eventually the German eagle becomes impatient with their usurpation and reduces them to their original abject state. The work is hardly amusing. It is, in fact, to some extent similar to part of Hutten's *Ad Caesarem Maximilianum ut bellum in Venetos coeptum prosequatur exhortatorium*. As the title indicates, it was not written as satire but as an oratorical effort to urge the fickle emperor into further war. The two works are rather close in their treatment of the rise of the Venetians, as a comparison of the first 58 lines of the *Piscatura* with lines 77-201 *passim* from the *Exhortatorium* would show (Böcking, III, 289-291 and 127-132).

No superior to the *Piscatura* as satire but rather even more virulent is the *Triumphus Capnionis*, which fairly foams with rabid hatred, while we the onlookers gape more amazed than amused at the spectacle. It is the most blatant instance of satire reduced to ire in all of Hutten's works and justifies like nothing else the charge of grimness and austerity. In this connection, however, there is an important point to consider: Like the *Eov*, written also against the enemies of Reuchlin, the *Triumphus* was published under a pseudonym, and the matter of authorship still poses some unanswered questions, even though Hutten's good friend Eoban Hessus wrote to Johann Lange, probably soon after the work was published: "Now you can be sure it was Hutten triumphing for Capnion. At first I didn't recognize his style, but as soon as I had gone further our Hutten became Eleutherius, because in truth he is free. I assume there were many reasons (which we can easily guess at) why he wore a mask and didn't want to be seen openly. No doubt about it. It's really Hutten. I swear by all that's greatest: Hutten's it is."[5] Joachim Camerarius, speaking later of Hutten in his biography of Philip Melanchthon, states, "By him is the triumphal poem about the victory of Reuchlin...."[6] Let us, nevertheless, examine the matter of authorship more closely.

In 1514 a *Triumphus Capnionis* appeared in manuscript under the name of Accius Neobius.[7] Barring error on the part of Mutianus Rufus, the actual author was not Hutten but Hermann von dem Busche. Prefixed to the work was an epigram by Hutten.[8] Whether the latter had any part at all in the composition of this *Triumphus* cannot be determined, though Erasmus in his *Spongia* gives us to understand that it was altogether Hutten's. He writes, "I was not the cause of Hutten's becoming an enemy of Hochstraten. He had written the *Triumphus* against him [Hochstraten] before he saw me or knew me, and on my advice he suppressed this work for two years."[9] This statement is contradicted both by Mutian's remark (note 8), however, and by an earlier comment of Erasmus himself, in the letter to Hutten of April 23, 1519. There he writes, "We haven't seen the *Triumphus* yet. It was nice that they suppressed it so long on our advice, and I don't doubt that they have toned down the contents."[10] His use of "they" in addressing Hutten implies that the 1514 version, as well as the final one, was not the latter's work. In 1514 it was Hutten, however, who was about to publish the piece and who withdrew it at Erasmus's behest.[11]

At the end of 1518 the work was finally released, under the name Eleutherius Byzenus now, with no epigram but with a preface and an epilogue. The publisher seems to have been Anshelm of Hagenau.[12] That it was actually Hutten who was responsible for the printing we do not know,[13] but since he did add the preface and the epilogue,[14] it was probably he who sent the manuscript to Anshelm. In view of the fact that he withdrew the piece in 1514 at Erasmus's request and promised to accede to the latter's wishes in everything (note 13), there must have been some particularly compelling reason for his apparent change of mind in 1518.

A point which has not been given due consideration in discussions of the authorship of the *Triumphus* leads us further into these obscurities. At the close of his letter to Pirckheimer from Bologna, May 25, 1517, Hutten adds the deceptively simple remark, "We haven't yet seen *Capnion's Triumph*. Send it."[15] We know that he was well acquainted with the 1514 version. He had contributed an epigram to it, and he had shown it to Erasmus. Why, then, did he write in 1517 that he had not yet seen the work? Unless, of course, it was not the same *Triumphus*. His request – perhaps also the change in pseudonym – indicates that in the intervening two years (and no doubt only shortly before) someone other than himself had revised the piece. It must have been the new version, still in manuscript form, that Pirckheimer was to send. Probably sometime in later 1517, then, after returning to Germany, Hutten wrote the preface, along with the epilogue and his revision of the work itself.[16]

An interesting question now arises: Who might

the mysterious figure be who must have reworked the *Triumphus* earlier in that year and caused Hutten to break his word to Erasmus, showing even more enthusiasm than he seems to have felt for the original version? One possibility is the same person who wrote the appendix to *Eov II*. The letters of this appendix were published in 1517 and thus probably composed about the same time as the *Triumphus* was revived and revised. The last of these letters, furthermore, drops the satiric mask and gives vent to openly strong invective akin to the spirit of the *Triumphus*. Merker has argued forcefully that Nikolaus Gerbel, an enthusiastic supporter of Reuchlin, was the author of the *Eov II* appendix, and this point Bömer has been willing to concede.[17]

As with the *Eov*, the problem of the authorship of the *Triumphus* will remain shrouded in uncertainty, but there is at any rate reason to believe that Hutten only put the latter work in its final form, after someone else – perhaps Nikolaus Gerbel – had revised the original version, done evidently by Hermann von dem Busche, and that Hutten was thus not solely responsible for its scurrilous abuse. As Erasmus's statements quoted above on p. 48 (notes 9 and 10) show, the 1514 version attacked Hochstraten and was violent, and Mutian (note 7) says that it was written against the Cologne theologians, so that it must not have been vastly different from the final version.

As for caricature in the work, we find that it gives way to a procession of horrors, chief of which is the atrocity committed on the apostate Jew Pfefferkorn, who caused all of Reuchlin's trouble. He is maimed with loving detail and used as a bloody broom on the streets of Pforzheim, the scene of the liberals' triumph (Gerbel's and Reuchlin's home town), dragged on a hook, while thousands cheer the ebbing of his life in agony. Even Böcking, Hutten's staunchest admirer, cries out in protest at this outrage: "I wonder how such repulsive and odious things could please anyone but a hangman and how the poet failed to see that Pfefferkorn would win favor with humane readers because of the boundless cruelty."[18]

The piece does have light, even happy, passages – those expressing joy at Reuchlin's accomplishments and his success over his enemies (actually never quite realized) – but they are not humorous. In the treatment of the theologians who comprise part of the procession there is some sarcasm, as,

> They're all convinced that they're the only ones who know
> What's true, what's false, what isn't right. They're more informed
> Than Phoebus's tripod, Delos, and Dodona's birds.
> If hornèd Hammon spoke to broiling Africans
> In Libyan sands, his words were not so true..."[19]

and these theologians are caricatured by means of their gods and weapons, carried on display (pp. 427-430).

Caricature becomes overdrawn grotesquerie with

at least two more of the principal figures, though. Hochstraten, the Cologne inquisitor, is made a fiery demon obsessed with his own element:

> ... he'll call for flames, shout "To the fire!"
> If something's judged correct, "The fire!" if wrong, "The fire!"
> If what you do is right, "The fire!" if not, "The fire!"
> He's fiery head to foot; he eats and swallows fire.
> His lung is fiery; through his throat he breathes out flames.
> His maw and liver glow with fire; he burns all things.
> The words he speaks are flames, and flames are what he writes.
> He always utters "Fire," his first and final word.
> His nose is fiery; fiery are his eyes; his heart
> Is made of charcoal. Scarcely he refrains in chains
> From shouting "Fire!" He wants this triumph, too, to burn," etc. (p. 432).

Ortvinus Gratius becomes a wretched poetaster with hellish, bewitching orbs: "Come, lictor, bind his eyes, lest all be hypnotized" (pp. 432-434). What a contrast to *Phalarismus*, where, as we shall see, a monster is made laughable! Here some obscurantists are only made monstrous. Others are merely berated: Arnold von Tungern is tongue-lashed for inordinate ambition, while Bertram von Naumburg is called a glutton, Bartholomäus Zehender, a viper, and Peter Meyer, a vain, ignorant hypocrite (pp. 434-436 and 438-441).

To pass now from the *Triumphus* and Hutten's caricature in verse to that in his dialogues, we discover in *Aula* another example of attack more through denunciation and bizarrerie than clever burlesque. A strange composition, it reads like an expression of heartfelt animosity but was evidently composed as a rhetorical exercise, since Hutten repeatedly assures us that he wrote it merely as a joke.[20] Though he complained about being at court, he admired Archbishop Albrecht and cannot have been as miserable as the dialogue implies.

Otto Flake calls the *Aula* a "Hofsatire,"[21] but its vituperative tone is rarely raised to the level of humor. What actual satire it contains, moreover, is, apart from some sarcasm, caricature that has become bitter and contemptuous. Describing the kind of person who is successful at court, Misaulus ("Hater-of-Court") says in part:

> Furthermore, princes are most foolish about choosing their attendants. Courtiers are selected not for their virtues but for their size – for broad shoulders, long legs, and high neck. It helps to have a terrifying beard or hair treated with the curling iron and to swagger on entering the court, throwing one's arms and legs about as though demanding those Virgilian boxing-gloves for a match with Entellus. Courtiers should also wear varicolored clothes decorated all over, gaudier than a cock with thirty hens, even

though such Thrasos aren't up to satisfying one woman's desire.[22]

Hyper-naturalistic descriptions of the filthiness at court reach the exaggerated proportions of caricature but nauseate rather than titillate—a point which calls for a short digression. In his book on Gerbel, Merker pays Hutten this flattering compliment: "So kraftvoll Hutten in seinen Satiren den Gegner anfaßt, so witzig und höhnisch sein Spott sein kann, er bleibt doch immer der Aristokrat, der sich von der derb-obszönen Komik der Fastnachtsspielfarçen und anderer Äußerungen des volkstümlich groben Geschmacks fernhält."[23] While it is true that Hutten's works, apart from the *Eov* (and, despite the question of authorship, Merker should at least have made an exception of them), show much less vulgarity than one is used to with writers of the period, we cannot rightly go so far as to say that Hutten held himself completely aloof from it. Yet Heinrich Grimm, at one point, is in total agreement with the view expressed by Merker. After mentioning the grossness of German towns and universities in Hutten's day, he adds: "Muß man es ihm [Hutten] unter solchen Umständen nicht zum besonderen Lobe werden lassen, zu besonderer Ehre anrechnen, daß er, im Gegensatz zu der gesamten zeitgenössischen Literatur, sich niemals in obszönen Scherzen oder platten Zoten erging und gefiel?"[24] Such a remark is not completely false, but it would lead one to believe that Hutten was a paragon of fastidiousness, when in fact he was not. There are, of course, the *Eov* to bear in mind, though the two epistles which we can with some confidence definitely ascribe to Hutten are not off-color. Later in his book Grimm does acknowledge that the *Eov* depend upon vulgar eroticism for much humorous effect.[25]

Let us leave the *Eov* aside, however. *Phalarismus* closes with the coarsest kind of insult, if decorously understated,[26] and in the *Praedones* Hutten conducts himself like a *Landsknecht*. Threatening the merchant who dares to impugn his respectability as a knight, he exclaims: "I'll tell you rightly, truly, and veraciously; unless you come to your senses and control your impudence, with my fists I'll smash these cheeks and all of your face, then knock out your teeth and bash in your ribs till you lie half dead in the mud, excreting pepper by the pound with half an ounce of saffron!"[27]

Strauß, for his part, seems to summarize the matter more accurately by saying, "Seine [Hutten's] Schriften zwar zeigen sich, wenn wir seinen Anteil an den Dunkelmännerbriefen abrechnen, wo aber Schmutz und Zoten durch den satirischen Zweck gefordert waren, merkwürdig rein, und insbesondere seine Briefe unterscheiden sich hierin vorteilhaft von manchen andern Briefwechseln jener Zeit."[28] While we should concede that Hutten's language is, all in all, worthy of a poet laureate of the Empire, still, as Böcking remarks in regard to the *In sceleratissimam Ioannis Pepericorni vitam ... exclamatio*, " ... even heroes are sons of their age."[29]

Coming back to *Aula*, we find this to be true when Hutten depicts dining-hall horrors that would have made a delicate courtier renounce eating. Inspired, no doubt, by Aeneas Sylvius (in the *De curialium miseriis*), he has Misaulus harangue disgustedly against the living conditions of a prince's attendants, saying in part: "Those who come to eat smell of yesterday's binge and eructate something odiously fetid. Someone sits with feculent thighs and vinous belly or vomits at the table." Toward the close of his tirade Misaulus exclaims, "Add to this the beds not merely impure but often pestilential, where a few days ago someone consumed by syphilis slept and where a leper sweated, the covers in which they tossed and turned and which they soaked with pus having been washed six months before."[30]

Since Hutten calls *Aula* a joke, he may have intended for this Grobianism and crassness to be read as caricature; and since Erasmus's friend Johann Froben refers to the work as "a most charming dialogue,"[31] Hutten's contemporaries may in fact have been amused by this hyperbolic coarseness, however much his modern readers turn away with loathing. At the same time, it was perhaps only a negative reaction that Hutten wanted to elicit at all. We cannot definitely say that Misaulus's censorious speech is an instance of the author's humor. Here, certainly, as in the whole of *Aula*, anger is the moving force, even though in the employ of rhetoric.

In the dialogue *Bulla* Hutten chooses a representative of the Church as an object of his wrath. Whereas in *Inspicientes* we are to find a papal legate caricatured, here the victim is a haughty papal bull, a bull which is, as we have seen, also a bubble and which ends by bursting after Hutten beats her, as she has belabored Liberty. Such lowbrow fisticuffs, the approach of an army of *Curtisanen* who are quickly routed by the arrival of Sickingen and the emperor with an escort, plus the explosion of Bulla make the dialogue action-packed but do not improve the caricature. At one point, however, the author does lift his satire to a more intelligent level. From the standpoint of humor the climax of the work comes when Bulla unwittingly burlesques the Church's trade in religious liberties by proclaiming exaggerated rewards for anyone who comes to her aid. Her appeal reads partly in this manner:

> Is anyone willing to protect Leo's daughter, oh pious folk, oh Christians, and slay this wretch [Hutten] with impunity? You'll get as your reward from Leo X five-thousand ducats paid in full by the Camera and a sinecure Benefice amounting to three-hundred gulden annually. In addition you'll get complete remission of all sins, and indulgences for two-thousand years, plus fifty-six carenes, and will be a Protonotary with the power to legitimatize bastards and create Counts Palatine. Also you can mortally sin once every day, be free from confession for the next seven years, and thereafter need confess but

once every seven years. I take that back. You'll only have to confess once as long as you live, except on the point of death. If you're not interested in benefices, you can marry your step-daughter, grand-daughter, or cousin, and if you make an oath, regardless of what it is, you don't have to keep it. If you make a deal, you can renege whenever you want. Whoever's been ex-communicated, whether by law, canon, or individual decree, for whatever reason, because of whatever deed however heinous, whoever has committed incest or adultery, has raped virgins or matrons, whoever has perjured himself, murdered, or apostatized – repeatedly, even – whoever has killed a priest, whoever has transgressed against all law human and divine, be absolved and innocent. Whoever has taken sacred objects or plundered temples can enjoy the spoils forever and won't be forced to return them. Hear ye, wherever you are, you haters of God and you who're devoid of humanity, for a small job here you can cleanse yourselves of the filthiest sins – just by killing this fellow, as anyone can do with impunity" etc.[32]

This one passage contrasts starkly with the general want of sophistication in what Paul Kalkoff calls "jener ergötzliche Ringkampf."[33]

With these dialogues *Aula* and *Bulla*, along with the *Triumphus* and the caricatures of the Venetians, we have surveyed Hutten's poorer productions in the genre. *Phalarismus*, by contrast, shows that he could be a master of ridicule through exaggeration. For a proper appreciation of this work it is necessary to have in mind the historical facts on which it is based. As in all good caricature, there is enough verisimilitude here to convince us that the satire is justified, with enough distortion to make the subject of it risible. In this work we find Hutten's most successful balance of fact with fiction.

Covetous of his young *Stallmeister*'s wife, Ulrich, duke of Württemberg, murdered her unsuspecting husband in May 1515. The victim, Hutten's cousin Hans, had served Ulrich well. His father Ludwig, furthermore, had loaned the duke 10,000 gulden interest-free (which had not been repaid) and had sent troops to help quell a peasant revolt. The murder was Ulrich's requital for all the service of Ludwig and his son. As though Hans had died in disgrace, the duke put a noose around the neck of the corpse. Adding further insult to injury, he refused to let his victim's family have the body. Hans's wife stayed on at court, while the duke's wife Sabine, Emperor Maximilian's niece, fled to her brothers in Bavaria. Ulrich agreed to the mildly punitive stipulations of the Treaty of Augsburg of October 1516 but soon afterwards broke his word. Such are the elements of this sordid tale important for *Phalarismus*.

The situation in the dialogue is this: The duke, having been approached by the ancient tyrant Phalaris in a dream, is led to Hades by Mercury, in order to converse with the Sicilian and learn some fine points of fiendishness. The work opens at the edge of Acheron, where Charon is about to ferry across the messenger god and his charge, called simply "Tyrannus." Mercury explains how Phalaris is concerned that Germany finally get a tyrant like other nations. Charon is amazed: "In Germany a tyrant?" He orders his fare to grab an oar, provoking haughty indignation. When Charon repeats the order, Tyrannus snarls, "You would never say that in Germany, and how I wish you would!" Charon threatens to smash him over the head with a pole if he refuses to cooperate. Because he is not an airy shade, Tyrannus has to pay more for the trip. "He won't mind," says Mercury. "He's a lavish squanderer." Having passed over the river and found the abode of Phalaris, Mercury leaves Tyrannus in the arms of his proud preceptor, to return for him later.

Tyrannus relates the incidents of Hans von Hutten's death, and Phalaris replies that he never thought of doing anything so beastly himself. He killed only suspected enemies. "In this I have to yield to you," he says, "a veteran tyrant to a novice." Tyrannus adds that because the victim had no mother to mourn for him, he (Tyrannus) was afraid that a full measure of satisfaction would be denied him. "But the father's mourning was tremendous," he exclaims. He goes on to mention further events connected with the murder, such as his refusal to let Hans's family give the corpse a proper burial and the Treaty of Augsburg, which he says he is flaunting. "Splendid!" declares the tutor. "A tyrant must be perfidious."

The conversation shifts to Tyrannus's wife. "I hated her passionately. I don't know why. She was lovely and charming, as well as highborn, and my family had no greater asset. Still, I despised her," he confesses. "It's common for tyrants to want, fear, and hate much without knowing why," Phalaris sagely notes. "So I decided to murder her as soon as I finished some other business," continues Tyrannus. "She got away, though." Phalaris observes that his pupil would thus be a ravenous wolf. "As you say," replies Tyrannus.

After the latter relates how he has suborned a number of knights, including Franks ("everything's for sale in Germany now"), has put them under his henchmen, and plans to make war, he asks Phalaris to give him some pointers on how to continue. The master suggests a number of exquisite tortures, at mention of which Tyrannus becomes enraptured. "Especially," warns Phalaris, "don't believe in any gods, hold tyranny to be the greatest good, and cultivate cruelty." "That's in my blood," Tyrannus responds. "For that I don't need a teacher." At the close of the conversation Phalaris admonishes Tyrannus to be more prudent in the future in disposing of paramours' husbands: "You botched the job on that Frank, you know," and the apprentice replies, "Yes, I was carried away. Voluptuousness got the best of me ...."

After being introduced to the other tyrants and told to brand the cheek of Hans von Hutten's father-in-law for prostituting his daughter, Ulrich is shown to his uncle, who, it is explained, has wayward ways of entertaining himself. Mercury returns, and the dialogue ends.[34]

Hutten stops at nothing in this vicious lampoon – nothing, that is, short of outright invective. In happy contrast to the *Triumphus*, *Phalarismus* is devastating without being denunciatory. Neither the author nor any of his characters attacks the duke. Ulrich, instead, is made to demolish himself. Needless to say, the best caricature is always of this kind. In *Phalarismus* Hutten's artistry, moreover, fails him no more than his wit. Well constructed, and with the usual lively and fluent dialogue, this work deserves to be recognized as a masterful piece of satire, despite the less favorable view expressed by several earlier critics.[35]

Almost as effective as the caricature of Ulrich is that of Cajetan in *Inspicientes*. In the last eight pages of the work[36] he appears as an arrogant little tyrant, shouting up at Sol that he ordered sunshine for the duration of his stay in the frigid North, and that for ten days he has had no ray of warmth. When Sol remarks that he was not aware of needing to obey the whims of mere mortals, Cajetan informs the god that as legate he has all the power of the pope to bind or loose on earth or in heaven. Sol replies that he has never believed papal claims. For that Cajetan threatens to send him straight to the devil unless he begs for forgiveness and does penance. This means, he explains, that Sol would have to fast several days, do some kind of labor, make a pilgrimage, give alms, or even be flogged. Sol remarks that the fellow must be insane. For that blasphemy he is excommunicated, *de facto*.

Cajetan renews his order for sunshine, and this time Sol says that he would have complied, but he thought it better not to shed any light on the shady dealings of the legate. Cajetan sees the wisdom of this policy and orders Sol to keep Germany in the dark. Furthermore, he wants it fogged up so that pestilence will vacate some prebends and bring more money into the papal coffers. After mutual reviling Sol rides away with Phaethon.

By treating a god in such a highhanded manner Cajetan becomes an absurd buffoon. While we laugh, however, we are bothered by one small point. We know that in reality the cardinal was not so overweening as to justify Hutten's burlesque. Caricature, as has been observed in the case of *Phalarismus*, should have verisimilitude. Basically it should be true to life; otherwise it is not appropriate to the subject. With the duke of Württemberg Hutten's caricature is highly pertinent, and enough fact is included to remind us that Ulrich was indeed an unprincipled reprobate. We laugh with satisfaction to see his depravity exaggerated to the point of absurdity. With Cajetan, on the other hand, we feel that Hutten is being unfair. We should perhaps see in this caricature, as in earlier description of the legate in *Inspicientes* (pp. 277-282), not the man himself, however, but the attitude of the institution which he represented. It may not have been that individual whom Hutten despised so much as the Church in general, for which Cajetan stood and for which he served as a scapegoat.

Before moving to our second group of Hutten's caricatures – those of himself – we might do well to take stock quickly of what we have found in this first assortment. While all satire is combative to some extent, part of what we have seen so far in this section tends to become impatient with the rapier of ridicule and to abandon it for the bludgeon of billingsgate. The epigrams included are rather light satire, to be sure. Heavier and more spiteful are *Marcus* and, especially, *De piscatura Venetorum*. As for *Phalarismus* and the caricature of Cajetan, while they are successfully comic, they are certainly vengeful. The *Triumphus*, *Aula*, and *Bulla* fully support the negative implications of the critical comments cited in the Introduction. When we examine Hutten's caricature of himself, however, we find again that those remarks become less than adequate. With this expression of his humor we re-enter a more jovial atmosphere. Anger and vindictiveness are again gone. The vicious tiger is once more a playful kitten.

In his biography of Konrad Celtis, Lewis Spitz writes, "Most of the humanists lacked real humor. They mocked a great many things human and divine. They seldom laughed at themselves."[37] Spitz does not say whether Hutten should be included in this group, but if the ability to laugh at one's self is the mark of "real humor," then Hutten possessed it. He seems to have been well aware of his own potential as a comic figure, and he uses himself for a laugh in a surprising number of instances, a few of which we have already seen. To mention two or three more before we consider the caricatures in *Fortuna* and *Febris II*, Hutten makes himself comical in the dialogue *Praedones* with his hot-footed impatience to have the Romanists reprehended. When Sickingen observes that there are four classes of robbers in Germany, Hutten leaps into the conversation with his exclamation, "Of which, host, the first and most pernicious is that of the Priests."[38] When Sickingen has begun denouncing the second class of robbers, the merchants, Hutten protests, "You're not leaving anything, host, to say afterwards against my *Curtisanen!*"[39] In the dialogue *Monitor II* he has himself characterized as a *persona non grata:* Monitor remarks to Sickingen, "... they say you're one of Luther's faction and are fostering that Hutten at home, who's going to be the cause some day of the greatest evils."[40] Otto Harnack may be right in suspecting that Hutten is meant in *Phalarismus* when, in reference to the torture by which a roasted man is given water to sprinkle on himself, only to aggravate his pain, Tyrannus says, "That's certainly exquisite, and I'll remember it. I've got somebody that punishment would suit."[41] Harnack remarks, "Bei diesen letzten Worten hat Hutten sicherlich in launiger Ironie an sich selber gedacht, der tatsächlich damals von Spähern des Herzogs verfolgt wurde."[42]

Throughout the dialogue *Fortuna* he casts himself in the role of a veritable fool. This work, being one of Hutten's most enjoyable, has provoked considerable comment, but little if any attention has been given to the fact that in it the author makes great sport of himself. Critics have been more interested in Hutten as a philosopher here than as a good-natured comedian who does not shrink from displaying himself on a pillory. Olga Gewerstack (*Lucian und Hutten*, p. 77) writes, "In dem Dialog 'Fortuna' lernen wir Hutten von einer ganz neuen Seite kennen, in einer Eigenschaft, der wir kaum mehr begegnen werden – das ist Hutten als Philosoph." Yet this role is a minor one and one which Hutten does not play with polish. The fact that he mentions Fortuna often in his writings is no sign that he ever thought deeply about the nature of chance and Providence, and his conclusion on this subject in the dialogue seems rather an indication of the contrary.

Regarding his portrayal of the goddess, much has been suggested as influence. Hutten definitely drew from the *Tabula Cebetis*, as pointed out by Grimm (p. 122) and Gewerstock (pp. 77-78), and he must have had Lucian in mind, as Gewerstock (pp. 77-89) and Bauer (*Philologus*, LXXV, 441-443) demonstrate by listing a number of similarities in technique and motifs. Possible is the influence of Erasmus's *Encomium moriae*, suggested by Paul Held (pp. 91-92), along with that of Petrarch's *De remediis utriusque fortunae*, which Hajo Holborn mentions (*Ulrich von Hutten* [Leipzig, 1929], p. 71), and even the description of Fortuna in

Aeneas Sylvius's letter of June 26, 1444, to Prokop von Rabstein, as Gewerstock again suggests (p. 30). While still other minor sources could be cited, there is one influence which seems to have been even more fundamental to Hutten's composition of *Fortuna* than Lucian's *The Dream* and *The Ship*. That is the Tenth Satire of Juvenal. A quick résumé of each work will indicate their similarity.

The Tenth Satire is about prayer. "What should we pray for? That is its theme," says Gilbert Highet.[43] Just as we do foolish things, we also pray for them, and it is not improper of the poet to exhort us to moderate our wishes with prudence.

> ... and what with reason do we fear
> Or do we long for? Have you ever made a plan
>   That seemed most promising yet didn't cause
>   regret? (11. 4-6)

Through a series of examples Juvenal makes graphic the sad truth that all too often we pray for what is in the long run injurious. Wealth, power, military glory, longevity, beauty – they are all better avoided than sought. Indeed, it is not necessary for us to pray at all, he closes. The gods know what we need:

> If my advice you want,
> You'll leave it to the gods to give us what they know
> Is suitable for us and right for our affairs (11. 346-348).

Man is dearer to the gods than to himself. If we must pray, it is enough to ask for a sound mind in a sound body. We should petition for mental fortitude and should be eager for work:

> Request a stalwart mind that lacks all fear of death
> And thinks longevity the least of nature's gifts,
> That's capable of standing any kind of work,
> That knows no anger, wants for nothing, valuing
> The labors and ordeals of Hercules far more
> Than Venus and the feasts of Sardanapalus
> (11. 357-362).

In the final two lines Juvenal makes an important statement about Fortuna (having earlier referred to her in passing). If we were prudent, she would be dishonored. Her venerableness is but a figment of our folly:

> Divine you wouldn't be, Fortuna, were men wise.
> We make a goddess of you, placing you on high
> (11. 365-366).

Hutten's dialogue shares the same theme and develops essentially this same conclusion, namely that we should be indifferent to fortune altogether. It opens *in medias res*. Hutten has come to the goddess to beg for special treatment. He wants first of all a comfortable salary – something which the rich can spare. Fortuna explains that the rich need all that they can get and have nothing left over for anyone else. Hutten wants, though, just enough for a life of leisure. This, he explains, consists of wife, home, gardens, villas with fish ponds, hunting dogs, and a few horses, so that one can go out occasionally; then servants, custodians, livestock, and at home, besides furniture, a portico, a library, dining rooms, sweating rooms, and baths; for the lady of the house clothes and jewelry. Finally, enough to provide for the children abundantly. All of this is to be used with splendor but not extravagantly. Such would be modest comfort, he thinks. Fortuna explains that the Fuggers are clamoring for a great deal more, and that if she were to start heeding demands for special favors, they would come first.

The conversation then turns to Fortuna herself, who says that she is blind because she used to reward the good but that they were being corrupted by her kindness. Jove, in taking the simplest corrective measures, put out her eyes. She goes on to say that Hutten should not look to the gods for favors but should strive on his own to build the life that he wants. As far as Jove is concerned, the only prayer worth praying is for a sound mind in a sound body.

After the discussion of Providence Fortuna instructs Hutten in the virtue of hard work. She also advises him to stay poor, since riches would distract him from study and would greatly increase his cares. Has he ever seen anyone with great wealth live in tranquillity, she asks. "Priests," says Hutten, whereupon Fortuna explains that

Jove punishes them with gout, fevers, rheumatism, dissension, envy, and concubines. "And you want wealth," she adds, "the clear path to that kind of life...." Hutten repeats that he wants only enough to live comfortably.

At his request the goddess dispenses some vicissitudes from her cornucopia. Charles becomes emperor, at which news the papal legate nearly hangs himself. Eager to find a wife, Hutten peeps into the horn, espying the girl of his dreams. She is scintillating with charms and has a tremendous dowry. What is more, she smiles at him. "At you, pretty as you are?" Fortuna asks sarcastically. "She's not the kind to care for looks," says Hutten. "She's admiring something else." Fortuna bids him stand back, gives the lass a toss from the wheel, and – oh, horrors! She lands in the lap of a pompous fop. What is even worse, the crops of the Huttens have been destroyed concomitantly. On the Steckelberg – the Huttens' fortress – fare will be scanty.

At this double calamity our hero becomes exasperated and loses all hope of succeeding with Fortuna. In the nearest chapel he will beg Christ for a sound mind in a sound body. "So, you've come to your senses at last," the goddess observes in her superior fashion. "To my great loss," moans Hutten, showing his disappointment. But Fortuna, far from being sympathetic, mocks him: "What are you waiting for? Is there another pretty girl smiling at you from my horn?" With her raillery ringing in his ears, Hutten departs in disgust.[44]

That the theme of this dialogue is taken principally from Juvenal seems very likely. Hutten comes to Fortuna with foolish requests, and she warns him away from them, recommending that satirist's simple prayer and hard work. Throughout the dialogue she has the part of Juvenal's wisdom and Hutten, that of the folly which Juvenal derides.

Hutten's intention of making himself a laughing-stock becomes further evident from the fact that he asks only for enough to live on in quiet comfort, which he then explains to be something far exceeding the bounds of modest retirement. He asks for an income of a thousand gulden per year, and he is ecstatic to discover that the girl in the cornucopia is wealthy (just as dowry was of some actual concern to him – see the letter to Arnold von Glauburg, Böcking, I, 287). Fortuna's scorn of both his looks and his disappointment shows also that he was not above letting himself be made the butt of a joke.

While *Fortuna* is a satire on the author, he is not the only object of ridicule in it. There are some slurs on representatives of the Church, including the pope, and the Fuggers are not spared, either; yet sharp satire and invective constitute but a relatively small part of this work.

In *Febris secunda* the reverse is true. We have already seen that Hutten makes use of irony and open censure here for one of his more extended sallies against the clergy. The caricature of himself dwindles proportionately, though it derives again in part from his desire for a wife (who Fever, like Fortuna, says would distract the scholar from his studies). As a matter of fact, Fever candidly states that Hutten is salacious. His desire keeps him from being prudent. She, however, can solve his problem: "I extinguish lust."[45] A little later (p. 135) she adds, after he has asked whether he should let her in and be sick for six months, as he was once from her visit: "You should give me twelve, a whole year, so that I might make you completely wise by taking away this concupiscence, which has hampered serious learning on your part for so long." Fever tells Hutten that she will make him pale and scholarly looking. He declines. "You used to want to be that way, so your teachers would call you studious; now you want to look healthy, so you won't displease the ladies, " she says. "But you're mistaken ..." (pp. 132-133). She notes that he has put on a little excess weight. She can take care of that problem, too, as well as give him a serious mien. Since he laughs and jokes so much, someone might suspect him of being fatuous (p. 134).

In other words, Hutten portrays himself again as something of a fool, this time a silly, fat, libidinous one. He does not deny the faults which Fever indicates. He protests merely that he does not want her "cure." Especially significant for us is the point that he laughed and joked a great deal. Through Fever, thus, Hutten pleads his own defense against charges of austerity. His self-caricature in *Fortuna* and in *Febris II* confirm the capacity for joviality for which we found evidence in Section III and in *Nemo*.

We have seen that he was a versatile, as well as erratic, caricaturist, producing quantities of crude burlesque but also some that is quite effective, and creating on occasion, especially where he himself is the subject, light, pleasant caricature along with the bitter travesties. As his irony is varied, so is his caricature, showing great range in tone and change in quality. Judging merely by the latter, we perceive that his humor is not so stereotyped as earlier critics would lead us to believe in their few brief remarks.

VI. CONCLUSION

The fundamental purpose of this examination of Hutten's comic writings has been to indicate that those scholars who have contributed to our better understanding of the man in other respects have neglected that more personable impression which he makes through some of his humor. Most students of his works have had nothing at all to say about his use of the comic, and the few who have have been blinded by his stringent satire to the point of overlooking the more jovial moments. Some of this lighter humor is also derisive, such as the epigram on the swearing of Bartolomeo d'Alviano cited in Section V, or *Nemo*, or the self-satire of *Fortuna* and *Febris II*. It is not true that all of his ridicule is motivated by that *saeva indignatio* charasteristic of a Jonathan Swift. Hutten wrote satire as vitriolic as Swift's and was probably at least as indignant when he wrote it. But whereas angry satire dominates his humorous writing, it does not comprise the sum total of it. That point can hardly be overemphasized. His personality was not straitjacketed. He did not have an obsessive mind that found amusement only in scorning enemies, personal and national. Nor was he so austere that he could not, and did not, relax in easy joking with friends or enjoy toying with words as he wrote. He found pleasure in humor as an end in itself, even to the extent of provoking merriment with his own potentially comic faults.

The idea of Hutten as merely cold, angry, and punitive – disposed to destroy but not to enjoy through humor – thus needs some revision. Flake

CONCLUSION

himself notes (p. 120) that the purely human side of the pugnacious, sardonic knight has been neglected. He writes, "Das herkömmliche Bild vom Polemiker und Politiker hat bewirkt, daß man Hutten zu einseitig sieht. Alles, was dazu dient, ihm menschlich und gefühlsmäßig näherzukommen, verdient Beachtung." Some of the material presented in this study should help to serve that purpose. It is through part of his comic writings that we come to know Ulrich von Hutten as a whole human being. Though he chaffed with the heat of indignation, he also laughed with the warmth of urbanity.

APPENDIX: THE PREFACE TO HUTTEN'S EDITION OF DE DONATIONE CONSTANTINI

Scholarly opinion has generally held that Hutten was ironic in praising Pope Leo X in the preface to his edition of Lorenzo Valla's *De donatione Constantini*,[1] that by the year 1517 he had too low an opinion of the pontiff to be sincere. Strauß states the matter this way: "Er [Hutten] hatte Leo X. während seiner bereits vierjährigen Regierung längst abgesehen, daß er in der Hauptsache ein Papst war wie die andern auch ...." Strauß goes on to cite as evidence the fact that Hutten "hatte schon im vorigen Sommer an Pirckheimer über ihn [Leo] als einen leichtgesinnten, geldgierigen Florentiner, einen Heiligen dessen Unheiligkeit bei allen Verständigen eine ausgemachte Sache sei, geschrieben."[2]

The date of this letter to Wilibald Pirckheimer is May 25, 1517. It antedates Hutten's preface to the edition of *De donatione Constantini* by some six months. To judge by appearances, then, Strauß is right. In fact, in the *Epistola ad Maximilianum Caesarem, Italiae ficticia*, written in July 1516, Hutten refers to Leo as a "Tuscan usurer," to whose "fraud" Rome was abandoned.[3] Here there is good reason to believe that Hutten was not expressing a heartfelt conviction, however. In this poem the figure Italy beseeches Emperor Maximilian for liberation from the forces which have ravaged her. Hutten naturally wanted to make her plight appear as pitiful as possible, since he was trying to stimulate the emperor to "rescue" her. For that reason he overlooked nothing that might contribute to the impression of abuse. To him at that time business men were contemptible, and the Medici were bankers. This is why we find here the words "Thuscus ... usurarius" and "Fluentino ... dolo."

There is even evidence that Hutten, when he cast this aspersion on Leo X, thought much better of the pope. Shortly before, he had composed a piece of verse addressed to Leo in which he laments the deplorable state of current affairs and begs the pope to pray for peace. In this poem, entitled *In annum M.D.XVI. prognosticon ad Leonem X. Pont. Max.* there is no hint of disparagement as Hutten directs urgent words not to a fraudulent financier but rather to a spiritual father.[4]

We have, thus, despite much criticism of the papacy as an institution and of the person of Pope Julius II, no clear evidence that Hutten bore any grudge against Leo X himself before May 1517, when he wrote the letter to Pirckheimer mentioned by Strauß. As we read this letter to the Nürnberg patrician, though, we discover something much stronger than the innuendo in Italia's rhetorical cry to Maximilian. Some event of particular importance must have taken place shortly before Hutten wrote to Pirckheimer in that May of 1517 for him to have become so truly angered at the pope.

To discover this event, we have only to look back to March 15 of the same year, at which time Leo issued a bull against the *Eov*. When we read the letter to Pirckheimer with this denunciation in mind, we are no longer at a loss to understand precisely why Hutten castigates the pope as he does. Because, for instance, he had believed Leo to favor Reuchlin's cause against Hochstraten, he saw in the bull the declaration of a monstrous change of heart. For this reason he calls Leo "lighter than any chaff, more fickle than any feather."[5]

The letter to Pirckheimer, then, is not an expression of long-felt hostility toward the pope. The anger it voices lasted into the summer of the same year, as Hutten's letter to Erasmus in July shows;[6] but we have no indication that Hutten was still harboring his ill will when he took service with the archbishop of Mainz, in the autumn of that year.

Cogent evidence of a return to a favorable opinion of the pope after becoming a courtier of the archbishop is to be found in the preface to *Triumphus Capnionis*, written, as we have seen (p. 49, above), probably in late 1517, or, in other words, at about the same time as the preface to *De donatione Constantini*. In the preface to *Triumphus Capnionis* Hutten calls Leo "most learned" and treats him warmly as an ally against the reactionary theologians, with whose stupidity, says Hutten, the pope is disgusted.[7] In the oration commonly called the *Türkenrede*, moreover, a work which dates from April and May 1518, Hutten likewise expresses approval of Leo, here as the restorer of papal dignity, though he chides him for the "Urbinense negotium" and roundly denounces the Curia.[8] In the preface to the *Türkenrede*, addressed to "Liberis omnibus ac vere Germanis," Hutten states expressly that he has held high regard for

Leo and that this is why he has dedicated to him his edition of Valla's book on the donation of Constantine.[9] From the summer of 1517 to the summer of 1519 there is no clear evidence that Hutten was opposed to Leo X, while these several references, along with the preface to *De donatione Constantini*, indicate the contrary.

The explanation for Hutten's good will toward the pope during this period might be sought chiefly in the influence of the archbishop of Mainz, in whose service Hutten was newly employed. Not until he was released from court in the summer of 1519 did he again show definite hostility toward Leo. In the dialogue *Vadiscus*, begun in that summer, Hutten twice denounces him indirectly, though we still find a weak echo of the former endorsement of the pope as the restorer of peace.[10] The dialogue *Fortuna*, which was also composed at this time, contains, as we have seen (p. 71), more unfavorable references to Leo, though he is not mentioned by name. In the preface to *De unitate ecclesiae conservanda*, probably written in October 1519,[11] Hutten expresses the hope that Leo will not completely disappoint him.[12] Since the pope did, Hutten is hostile toward him in subsequent writings.

Important to the case for sincerity in the preface to *De donatione Constantini*, which is central to the whole question of Hutten's attitude toward Leo X, is the dating of the work. December 1, 1517, is the composition date originally listed. In 1925, however, Paul Kalkoff, on the unproved assertion of

Otto Clemen and Oskar Brenner that Hutten's edition of *De donatione Constantini* did not appear until early 1520,[13] reasoned that the preface must have been written in 1519 and backdated.[14]

Josef Benzing in an article published in 1954 argued in turn for the original date.[15] He noted the statement of Beatus Rhenanus in a letter to Zwingli from March 19, 1519, ("Edidit et alia quaedam ad Leonem X. omnium mortalium audentissimus"), indicating that the work was at that time already published, and he further pointed out that we have no reason to doubt Hutten's having visited the Steckelberg (where he is supposed to have composed the preface) in late November and early December 1517, a matter which Kalkoff had challenged. In his book on Hutten published in 1956, however, Benzing recanted. Referring to his article, he wrote, "Nach [Heinrich] Grimms neuerem Forschungsergebnis ist der dortige Datierungsversuch nicht aufrechtzuerhalten. Hutten war im Dezember 1517 nicht auf Steckelberg, sondern in Frankreich. Die Datierung der Vorrede auf den 1. Dezember 1517 muß also eine bewußte Rückdatierung sein."[16]

This "Forschungsergebnis" of Grimm reads, "1517 war Hutten noch gar nicht imstande, eine so anklagende Praefatio wie die vorliegende zu formulieren. Im übrigen weilte er im Dezember 1517 in Paris (vgl. Böck. I, 162), von wo er erst Ende Januar 1518 in Mainz ankam. Huttens Schrift erschien frühestens Ende 1519."[17] On each point Grimm's argument is open to attack.

DE DONATIONE CONSTANTINI

The first is a restatement of the reasoning which Kalkoff thought would clinch the case for a later date. He wrote, "Entscheidend ... ist die Erwägung, daß er [Hutten] so kurze Zeit nach der Rückkehr aus Italien und ohne von dem kirchlichen Konflikt in Deutschland noch berührt zu sein, diese wuchtige und leidenschaftliche Anklage gegen das Papsttum zu formulieren noch gar nicht imstande war."[18] Yet not only does this claim rest on nothing factual; it is vitiated also both by the evidence that the preface was not written as the castigation which Kalkoff assumes, and by the fact that Hutten hardly penned a stronger denunciation of any pope than in that letter to Pirckheimer of May 25, 1517, from Bologna, before he had even left Italy.

Grimm's second point seems also to be derived from Kalkoff, who, in the note just cited, expresses doubt that Hutten was at the Steckelberg December 1. He does not, however, offer any real evidence, and Grimm's reference to Böcking is likewise insubstantial. We find on that page Budé's letter to Erasmus dated "die brumae" 1517, where the French humanist reports merely that he met Hutten shortly before in Paris. The date December 1 leaves Hutten ample time to have reached Paris from the Steckelberg and to have been seen by Budé before December 21.

Finally, Grimm's assertion, "Huttens Schrift erschien frühestens Ende 1519" is made doubtful not only by Beatus Rhenanus's statement, already cited, but also by the remark of Hutten himself in the "Liberis omnibus ac vere Germanis" referred to above, p. 79 (note 9). The composition date of this latter work is, according to Grimm himself, December 1518.[19]

Since Benzing sets as a *terminus a quo* for the publication of Hutten's edition of *De donatione Constantini* September 1518,[20] the work must have appeared in the autumn of the same year, so that a composition date for the preface of December 1, 1517, is not at all unlikely. Until stronger evidence is presented against it, the original date must stand. This date strengthens the likelihood of sincerity in the preface by placing it in the period of Hutten's entrance into service with the archbishop of Mainz, at the time when Hutten was otherwise writing very positively of Leo, as well.

Instead of supporting the generally accepted thesis that he very early became a bitter foe of Leo X, the available evidence indicates rather that Hutten did not do so before the middle of 1519. How conclusive we find much of this evidence depends, to be sure, on how willing we are to take him at his word, but the burden of proof lies with those who are not willing to do so. At any rate, since it is questionable that Hutten wrote the preface to his edition of *De donatione Constantini* as irony, the work should not be used to document any view of his satire.

NOTES: I. INTRODUCTION

[1] The word "humor" is construed throughout this study according to general American usage today as equivalent to the comic in general. Thus it does not exclude satire. The more traditional use of the word as a type of the comic is better avoided because of its greater impreciseness. Analyzing this meaning in his essay "Les définitions de l'humour," Fernand Baldensperger observes, with befitting skepticism, "Il n'y a pas d'humour, il n'y a que des humoristes. C'est, en somme, la conclusion de toute enquête poussée un peu loin à travers la diversité des manifestations et des définitions de cette variété du comique" *(Études d'histoire littéraire* [Paris, 1907], p. 217). Benedetto Croce explains, "Giacchè la varietà di quelle definizioni ha la sua buona ragione. Ognuno dei definitori ha avuto l'occhio ad uno o a più scrittori determinati; ed ha fissato il concetto dell' umorismo generalizzando alcune loro qualità che più lo cospiccano" ("L'Umorismo: Del vario significato della parola e del suo uso nella critica letteraria," *Journal of Comparative Literature*, I, no. 3 [1903], 226). As the word is used in this study, such subjectivity, it is hoped, will be circumvented. Other terms used here also conform to normal American usage today, with consideration given to any evident differences between this usage and Hutten's own terminology.

[2] Ulrich von Hutten, *Opera quae reperiri potuerunt omnia*, ed. Eduard Böcking. 5 vols. Leipzig, 1859-1861, reprinted Aalen, 1963. These works are cited in the following notes as "Böcking." In addition to these five volumes Böcking also edited a two-volume *Operum supplementum*, Leipzig, 1864-1870, reprinted Osnabrück, 1966.

[3] "Der Einfluß Lukians von Samosata auf Ulrich von Hutten," *Philologus*, LXXVI (1920), 192-207.

[4] *Germanic Review*, XXIII (1948), 18-29.

[5] *Ibid.*, p. 25.

[6] Böcking, II, 461.

[7] David Friedrich Strauß, *Ulrich von Hutten*, ed. Karl

NOTES: I

Martin Schiller (Meersburg and Leipzig, 1930), p. 197.
[8] *Ibid.*, p. 24.
[9] Walther Brecht, *Die Verfasser der Epistolae obscurorum virorum* (Straßburg, 1904), p. 364.
[10] *Ulrichs von Hutten Lehrjahre an der Universität Frankfurt (Oder) und seine Jugenddichtungen* (Frankfurt [Oder] and Berlin, 1938), p. 143.
[11] *Ulrich von Hutten* (Berlin, 1929), p. 164, from the chapter entitled "Die Dunkelmänner." Flake, too, bases his opinion largely on the *Eov*.

NOTES: II. THE EPISTOLAE OBSCURORUM VIRORUM

[1] Böcking, II, 460.
[2] *Ibid.*, p. 198.
[3] Aloys Bömer, *Epistolae obscurorum virorum*, I (Heidelberg, 1924), 107.
[4] Böcking, II, 277.
[5] Bömer, I, 85-87.
[6] Böcking, I, 125.
[7] Brecht, pp. 13-16.
[8] Bömer, I, 87.
[9] Böcking, I, 133.
[10] See Bömer, I, 109-110. Josef Benzing, in *Ulrich von Hutten und seine Drucker* (Wiesbaden, 1956), p. 136, no. 244, lists the date of the second edition of *Eov II* as "nach 1517" instead of "noch 1517."
[11] Bömer, II, 181.
[12] Böcking, I, 147-148. Hutten makes the same implication in the preface to *Triumphus Capnionis, ibid.*, p. 238: "Obscuris Viris laqueum praebui...." See also *ibid.*, p. 197, line 29, and Böcking's footnote.
[13] *Ibid.*, pp. 136-137.
[14] *Ibid.*, p. 150.
[15] *Ibid.*, p. 126.
[16] Strauß, p. 203.
[17] Böcking, III, 64.
[18] Brecht, pp. 290-293.
[19] Paul Merker, *Der Verfasser des Eccius dedolatus und anderer Reformationsdialoge* (Halle, 1923), pp. 302-303.
[20] *Zentralblatt für Bibliothekswesen*, XLI (1924), 5-6. See also Brecht, pp. 16-17.
[21] Bömer, *Ep. ob. vir.*, I, 92.
[22] Böcking, I, 105.
[23] Merker, pp. 309-311.
[24] *Ibid.*, pp. 305-307.
[25] Bömer, *Ep. ob. vir.*, I, 101-102.
[26] Böcking, I, 133.
[27] Brecht, p. 28. On p. 357 he does admit the possibility of Fuchs's, as well as Friedrich Fischer's, help.
[28] Böcking, I, 130.

[29] Brecht, p. 20.
[30] Böcking, II, 461. *Cf.* Brecht, p. 28.
[31] Brecht, p. 29.
[32] Böcking, II, 460.
[33] Brecht, pp. 5, 45, 274, and 357.
[34] Richard Newald, *Probleme und Gestalten des deutschen Humanismus*, ed. Hans-Gert Roloff (Berlin, 1963), p. 304.
[35] Bömer, *Ep. ob. vir.*, I, 93.
[36] Böcking, I, 150.
[37] *Ibid.*, p. 163.
[38] Bömer, *Ep. ob. vir.*, I, 90.
[39] Merker, p. 306.
[40] Bömer, *Ep. ob. vir.*, I, 91-92.

NOTES: III. HUTTEN'S USE AND APPRECIATION OF JOCULARITY

[1] Fife, p. 25.
[2] Böcking, V, 482-485.
[3] *Ibid.*, p. 406.
[4] *Ibid.*, III, 212:
"Iam pede pertaesum est claudoque insistere talo;
Qui valet ut vivat, me perimant Veneti."
[5] *Ibid.*, I, 26.
[6] *Ibid.*, p. 35.
[7] *Ibid.*, p. 422. Böcking mistakenly dates this letter 1520. See Alfred Hartmann, *Die Amerbachkorrespondenz*, II (Basel, 1943), 207, no. 699.
[8] Böcking, I, 274.
[9] *Ibid.*, III, 234. While he says it is unusual of Hutten to toy with words, Böcking elsewhere finds an instance of paronomasia where most readers would not. In the letter to Balthasar Fachus of August, 21, 1512, Hutten asks, "Sed tu quid agis? ducis an duceris? id est tot puellis Saxonibus unam tibi matrimonio (quod nuper aliqui susurrabant) conscribis, an caput radis, ut dignus fias coelestis boni ruminando? an hoc quod tu respondere solebas, Phachus manes?" (*Ibid.*, I, 26). In a footnote Böcking says, "Ludit ambiguis verbis *Fachus* et *vagus*, i.e. caelebs." This interpretation seems strained, particularly as Hutten elsewhere (*ibid.*, p. 205) writes, "... ita dabo operam enim, *Huttenus perpetuo ut sim* [italics mine], neve unquam desertor mei inveniar...."
[10] *Ibid.*, I, 216.
[11] *Ibid.*, p. 302.
[12] *Ibid.*, IV, 39.
[13] *Ulrichs von Hutten deutsche Schriften* (Straßburg, 1891), pp. 18-19.
[14] That Hutten derived his idea of Bulla's explosion from the *Narrenschneidenmotif* of the *Fastnachtsspiel* has been suggested along with the probability of Lucian's influence. In this connection see Olga Gewerstock, *Lucian und Hutten* (Berlin, 1924), p. 103, and Albert Bauer, "Der Einfluß Lukians von Samosata auf

Ulrich von Hutten," *Philologus*, LXXV [1918], 458. *Cf.* the ills of the protagonist in *Eccius dedolatus*. Another possible source of influence is Plautus's *Casina*, lines 325-326, where Olympio says of Lysidamus's wife Cleostrata, "Nunc in fermento totast, ita turget mihi," and Lysidamus responds, "Ego edepol illam mediam diruptam velim." As Bauer notes, however, the idea of the explosion is implicit in the word *bulla*. A very similar idea occurs also in the fourth oration against the duke of Württemberg. Addressing there the scelerate ruler, Hutten exclaims, "Quodsi tuam mentem perscrutatus quis fuerit tuasque cogitationes possit ad confessionem adigere, quantum, dii boni, scelerum, quantum pessimorum flagitiorum ex hoc sinuoso pectoris tui labyrintho acervatim effundes?" (Böcking, V, 73).

[15] Böcking, I, 175-176. In the letter to Pirckheimer of October 25, 1518, Hutten continues this word-play on *Nemo* and *Nihil*, though in bitter resentment at the criticism of jurists regarding the work *Nemo*, or more rightly, the preface. *Ibid.*, p. 211.

[16] Paul Held, in *Ulrich von Hutten. Seine religiös-geistige Auseinandersetzung mit Katholizismus, Humanismus, Reformation* (Leipzig, 1928), implies (p. 57) that Hutten identified with Nemo throughout the work itself and states (p. 43) that it was written as "Selbstsatire." This assumtion, however, is unlikely.

[17] Böcking, I, 176.
[18] *Ibid.*, p. 45.
[19] *Ibid.*, p. 174.
[20] *Ibid.*, pp. 213-214.
[21] Bömer, *Ep. ob. vir.*, II, 127.
[22] Böcking, I, 193-194.
[23] *Ibid.*, pp. 195-196.
[24] *Ibid.*, p. 273.
[25] *Ibid.*, pp. 286-287. See also Strauß, pp. 266-268.

NOTES: IV. HUTTEN'S IRONIC SATIRE

[1] Böcking, III, 269-270.
[2] *Ibid.*, p. 279, number 4.
[3] *Ibid.*, V, 73-74.
[4] *Ibid.*, p. 324.
[5] *Ibid.*, IV, 272.
[6] *Die Dialogliteratur der Reformationszeit* (Leipzig, 1905), p. 18.
[7] Böcking, IV, 83-86.
[8] In the letter written to Charles V in March 1521, for instance, Hutten states (*ibid.*, II, 44, line 22), "sed de me deus et Fortuna viderint...." Here the relationship between the two is not indicated, but in the letter to Eoban Hessus of July 21, 1523, written shortly before his death, Hutten exclaims: "Est tandem modus, Eobane, aut finis est improbae fortunae acerbissime nos persequenti? illi quidem esse non puto, sed nobis tantum animi est quantum ad illius ferendum insultus satis credi possit: *hoc unum nobis solatium, hoc praesidium reliquit qui cetera illius iniuriae permisit* [italics mine]" (*ibid.*, p. 252). Here the idea is clearly expressed that God rules supreme but has delegated to Fortune the control of mortal affairs. This concept is probably best known from Dante's treatment of it in the seventh canto of the "Inferno," lines 73 and following.
[9] Böcking, I, 218.
[10] *Ibid.*, p. 216.
[11] Heinrich Grimm (p. 142) theorizes that *Nemo I* was written "in der Zeit von Ostern 1507 bis März 1509."
[12] Böcking, I, 270.
[13] Grimm, p. 143.
[14] Böcking, III, 110.
[15] Held, p. 57, and Grimm, p. 141.
[16] Böcking, III, 112.
[17] One version derived from a monk named Radulfus and the other from a Straßburg barber, Jörg Schan. See Johannes Bolte, "Niemand und Jemand," *Shakespeare Jahrbuch*, XXIX-XXX (1894), 4-91, especially 8-21. The droll work of the late thirteenth-century monk

from Anjou was imitated in a variety of similar collections of Biblical statements containing the word "nobody." One of these is the *Sermo pauperis Henrici de sancto Nemine* which Otto Clemen published in *Theologische Studien und Kritiken* (1906), 308-312, after Bolte's edition in Alemannia, XVI (1888), 199-201. We do not have a definite date for the *Sermo*, but it had been printed by Hutten's time. Schan's German version dates from the late fifteenth century. Hutten refers to the Nemo-joke of Ulysses with Polyphemus (Böcking, III, 108-109 and 117), but Homer seems to have had little effect on him. To a humanist public an association with the Greek lent prestige, which mention of obscure medieval writers could only have impaired.

[18] Werner Kaegi, in "Hutten und Erasmus," *Historische Vierteljahrschrift*, XXII (1924-1925), 260-264, gives skepticism exaggerated importance in Hutten's development, making it the grounds for early congeniality with Erasmus.

[19] "Aber so plötzlich, wenn auch nicht unmotiviert, diese geistige Haltung bei Hutten auftritt, so rasch verschwindet sie wieder in seiner geistigen Gesamtentwicklung. Außer seiner zufälligen persönlichen Lage besaß er doch in seiner Charakteranlage zu geringe Voraussetzungen, um eine solche Skepsis festzuhalten und auszubauen" (p. 57).

[20] Strauß, p. 111.

[21] Grimm, p. 143. See also Böcking, III, 527, and Benzing, p. 105, no. 182.

[22] Böcking, IV, 35. On the eating of fish see Erasmus's dialogue *Ichthyophagia*.

[23] Böcking, IV, 113-114. *Cf. ibid.*, pp. 89-90.

NOTES: V. HUTTEN'S USE OF CARICATURE

[1] Böcking, III, 254-255, no. 120.
[2] *Ibid.*, p. 219, no. 28.
[3] *Ibid.*, p. 289.
[4] The epigrams which are similar to *Marcus* are (from the *Ad Caesarem Maximilianum epigrammatum liber*, *ibid.*, III, 207-268) nos. 15, 21, 23, 27, and 32.
[5] *Ibid.*, I, 240.
[6] Quoted by Böcking, *ibid.*, II, 362, note.
[7] Mutianus Rufus, in a letter of that year (*ibid.*, I, 31) writes, "... dabo Triumphum Capnionis ab Accio Neobio concinnatum in Colonienses theologistas...."
[8] In a letter of August 8, 1514 (*ibid.*, p. 32), Mutianus states, "Ostendit tibi [Eoban Hessus] solertissimus pater Urbanus ... Triumphum Neobii, id est Buschii, cui adhaeret Hutteni Epigramma extemporale."
[9] *Ibid.*, II, 274-275.
[10] *Ibid.*, I, 261: "Triumphum nondum vidimus. gratum erat quod nostro consilio tam diu presserint; nec dubito quin totum argumentum sint moderati."
[11] In a letter of August 25, 1517 *(ibid.*, p. 151), Erasmus states, "Ego ante biennium Triumphum Reuchlinicum, iam tum paratum editioni, in Germania premendum curavi...." See also note 13, following.
[12] Benzing, p. 58.
[13] Erasmus, who seems to have wanted to put the blame for the publication on Hutten, does not state specifically who the guilty party was. His presentation of the matter in *Spongia*, paragraphs 376-378 (Böcking, II, 318), reads as follows: "Quin ante hoc etiam tempus, quum Moguntiae primo colloquio mecum fabularetur, ostendit Reuchlini Triumphum, carmen sane elegans. Suasi ut premeret.... Post menses complures iterum me convenit Francfordiae; primo statim congressu rogabam ecquid meminisset consilii mei; respondit sese probe meminisse, neque quicquam sibi aeque decretum esse ac meo consilio parere in omnibus. deinde prodiit carmen una cum triumphali pictura sane quam magnifica, sed quae nihil aliud quam Capnionem gravaret invidia,

et adversarios provocaret satis sua sponte furentes ...."
[14] A good statement of the solid case for Hutten's authorship of these addenda is presented by Strauß, p. 169.
[15] Böcking, I, 135.
[16] With some confidence we can date the composition of the preface, at least, during this period. In it Hutten writes, "... cum anno abhinc tertio euntem Romam pecunia servitiis ac equis instructum Hogostratum, modestius fortuna uteretur frustra monerem ..." *(ibid.,* p. 236). In a note to p. 307 of his *Johann Reuchlin, sein Leben und seine Werke* (Leipzig, 1871, reprinted Nieuwkoop, 1964) Ludwig Geiger makes this observation: "Wann die Ankunft Hochstratens in Rom erfolgte, lässt sich nicht genau bestimmen; gewiss vor Ende September, wenn es wahr ist, was Hermann Busch aus Köln 30. Sept. 1514 an Reuchlin schreibt, dass die Dominikaner ihm [Hochstraten] aufs neue 1500 Goldgulden nach Rom geschickt hätten." That date must be a *terminus ad quem*, even if Busch was in error about the money sent. Surely he was not mistaken about Hochstraten's having left for Rome. Hutten must have met the inquisitor in the summer of 1514. Three years later would of course be summer or autumn, 1517. Grimm (Benzing, p. 4) ascribes the preface to "Frühjahr 1518," no doubt because of its similarity to the letter to Hermann von Neuenar dated April 3, 1518 (Böcking, I, 164-168). For Busch's letter to Reuchlin see Böcking, *Supplementum*, II, 746-747.
[17] Merker, pp. 292-296, and Bömer, *Zentralblatt für Bibliothekswesen*, XLI, 5 and 10, and *Ep. ob. vir.*, I, 102, note.
[18] Böcking, III, 437.
[19] *Ibid.*, p. 423.
[20] See *ibid.*, I, 211-212, 218, 220, and 248. Gulielmus Menapius writes in his letter to Amerbach, March 1, 1539, the preface to his own *Aula*, that Hutten must have been moved by something less than anger: "... nisi forte putabimus, quod ego libentius sequor, non punien-

di dolores sui, sed exercendi stili gratia lusisse ipsum in aulam" *(ibid.,* II, 468).
[21] Flake, p. 200: "Uns interessiert der Mut, der dazu gehörte, als Höfling Albrechts eine Hofsatire zu verfassen."
[22] Böcking, IV, 66.
[23] Merker, p. 43.
[24] Grimm, p. 70.
[25] *Ibid.,* p. 176.
[26] Böcking, IV, 25.
[27] *Ibid.,* p. 364.
[28] Strauß, p. 245. Referring to this statement, Flake, p. 68, advances the explanation that Hutten so concentrated on what he was doing that his mind never wandered: "Seine Aufmerksamkeit galt der Sache, der er gerade diente: auf Ausspannung legte er offenbar keinen Wert, er gehört nicht zu den gelassenen Naturen." The idea of austerity would seem to be carried to an extreme here.
[29] Böcking, III, 346, note to line 49.
[30] *Ibid.,* IV, 71-72. *Cf.* Erasmus's dialogue *Diversoria.*
[31] Böcking, I, 220.
[32] *Ibid.,* IV, 326.
[33] *Ulrich von Hutten und die Reformation* (Leipzig, 1920), p. 266. Kalkoff goes on to say: "... der Verfasser durfte in der Tat auf das klassische Gepräge seines witzigen Werkes (festivitas non inurbana) stolz sein." [For Hutten's phrase see Böcking, I, 436.]
[34] Böcking, IV, 4-25.
[35] See Niemann, p. 31; Kalkoff, p. 28; and Held, pp. 60-61.
[36] Böcking, IV, 301-308.
[37] *Conrad Celtis: The German Arch-Humanist* (Cambridge, Mass., 1957), p. 91.
[38] Böcking, IV, 367.
[39] *Ibid.,* p. 372.
[40] *Ibid.,* p. 350.
[41] *Ibid.,* p. 19.

NOTES: V

⁴² *Ulrich von Hutten*, in *Im Morgenrot der Reformation*, ed· Julius von Pflugk-Harttung (Basel, 1921), p. 490.
⁴³ *Juvenal the Satirist* (Oxford, 1962,) p. 125.
⁴⁴ Böcking, IV, 77-100.
⁴⁵ *Ibid.*, p. 131.

NOTES: APPENDIX. THE PREFACE TO HUTTEN'S EDITION OF DE DONATIONE CONSTANTINI

[1] Böcking, I, 155-161.
[2] Strauß, p. 212.
[3] Böcking, I, 108.
[4] *Ibid.*, III, 252-254. See also Benzing, p. 3.
[5] Böcking, I, 134.
[6] *Ibid.*, pp. 147-148.
[7] *Ibid.*, 237.
[8] *Ibid.*, V, 104-105.
[9] *Ibid.*, I, 241: "... optima mihi et aequissima semper omnia de Leone X. persuasi. quem tantum abest ut in hac re metuam, ut etiam Laurentii Vallae adversus ementitam Constantini donationem libellum in lucem iterum, praefatione ad ipsum facta edere nuper ausus sim...." See also Otto Harnack, p. 498, who considers this passage evidence for sincerity in Hutten's praise of Leo X.
[10] Böcking, IV, 154, 218, and 183.
[11] Hutten clearly implies in the letter to Hessus of October 26, 1519, that he has already written the preface in question: "dignum duxi adscribere praefationem quae simul edetur" (Böcking, I, 314). Grimm, Benzing, p. 8, states that it was written in November and December of that year.
[12] Böcking, I, 328-331.
[13] Martin Luther, *Werke: Kritische Gesamtausgabe*, L (Weimar, 1914), 65-66. *Cf.* "Briefwechsel," II (Weimar, 1931), 48-51.
[14] *Huttens Vagantenzeit und Untergang* (Weimar, 1925), p. 223, note.
[15] "Ulrich von Hutten und der Druck seiner Schriften in der Schweiz," *Stultifera Navis*, XI (1954), 70-71.
[16] *Hutten und seine Drucker*, p. 118.
[17] *Ibid.*, p. 3.
[18] *Vagantenzeit*, p. 223, note.
[19] *Hutten und seine Drucker*, p. 4.
[20] *Stultifera Navis*, p. 71.

BIBLIOGRAPHY

Baldensperger, Fernand. *Études d'histoire littéraire*. Paris, 1907.
Bauer, Albert. "Der Einfluß Lukians von Samosata auf Ulrich von Hutten," *Philologus*, LXXV (1918), 437-462, and LXXVI (1920), 192-207.
Benzing, Josef. "Ulrich von Hutten und der Druck seiner Schriften in der Schweiz," *Stultifera Navis*, XI (1954), 68-73.
— *Ulrich von Hutten und seine Drucker*, Beiträge zum Buch- und Bibliothekswesen, vol. 6. Wiesbaden, 1956.
Bömer, Aloys. *Epistolae obscurorum virorum*. 2 vols. Heidelberg, 1924.
— "Verfasser und Drucker der Epistolae obscurorum virorum: Kritik einer neuen Hypothese," *Zentralblatt für Bibliothekswesen*, XLI (1924), 1-12.
Bolte, Johannes. "Niemand und Jemand," *Shakespeare Jahrbuch*, XXIX-XXX (1894), 4-91.
Brecht, Walther. *Die Verfasser der Epistolae obscurorum virorum*, Quellen und Forschungen zur Sprach- und Culturgeschichte der germanischen Völker, vol. 93. Straßburg, 1904.
Clemen, Otto. "Zu Huttens Nemo," *Theologische Studien und Kritiken*, LXXIX (1906), 308-312.
Croce, Benedetto. "L'Umorismo: Del vario significato della parola e del suo uso nella critica letteraria," *Journal of Comparative Literature*, I, no. 3 (1903), 220-228.
Fife, Robert Herndon. "Ulrich von Hutten as a Literary Problem," *Germanic Review*, XXIII (1948), 18-29.
Flake, Otto. *Ulrich von Hutten*. Berlin, 1929.
Geiger, Ludwig. *Johann Reuchlin, sein Leben und seine Werke*. Leipzig, 1871, reprinted Nieuwkoop, 1964.
Gewerstock, Olga. *Lucian und Hutten*, Germanische Studien, vol. 31. Berlin, 1924.
Grimm, Heinrich. *Ulrichs von Hutten Lehrjahre an der Universität Frankfurt (Oder) und seine Jugenddichtungen*. Frankfurt (Oder) and Berlin, 1938.

BIBLIOGRAPHY

Harnack, Otto. *Ulrich von Hutten*, in *Im Morgenrot der Reformation*, ed. Julius von Pflugk-Harttung. Basel, 1921.
Hartmann, Alfred, ed. *Die Amerbachkorrespondenz*. 5 vols. Basel, 1942-1958.
Held, Paul. *Ulrich von Hutten. Seine religiös-geistige Auseinandersetzung mit Katholizismus, Humanismus, Reformation*, Schriften des Vereins für Reformationsgeschichte, Jahrgang 46, vol. 1 (No. 144). Leipzig, 1928.
Highet, Gilbert. *Juvenal the Satirist*. Oxford, 1962.
Holborn, Hajo. *Ulrich von Hutten*. Leipzig, 1929.
Hutten, Ulrich von. *Opera quae reperiri potuerunt omnia*, ed. Eduard Böcking. 5 vols. Leipzig, 1859-1861, reprinted Aalen, 1963.
— *Operum supplementum*, ed. Eduard Böcking. 2 vols. Leipzig, 1864-1870, reprinted Osnabrück, 1966.
Kaegi, Werner. "Hutten und Erasmus," *Historische Vierteljahrschrift*, XXII (1924-1925), 200-278 and 461-514.
Kalkoff, Paul. *Huttens Vagantenzeit und Untergang*. Weimar, 1925.
— *Ulrich von Hutten und die Reformation*, Quellen und Forschungen zur Reformationsgeschichte, vol 4. Leipzig, 1920.
Luther, Martin. *Werke: Kritische Gesamtausgabe*. Weimar, 1883 ff.
Merker, Paul. *Der Verfasser des Eccius dedolatus und anderer Reformationsdialoge*, Sächsische Forschungsinstitute in Leipzig, Forschungsinstitut für neuere Philologie, II. Neugermanistische Abteilung, vol. 1. Halle, 1923.
Newald, Richard. *Probleme und Gestalten des deutschen Humanismus*, ed. Hans-Gert Roloff. Berlin, 1963.
Niemann, Gottfried. *Die Dialogliteratur der Reformationszeit*, Probefahrten, vol. 5. Leipzig, 1905.
Spitz, Lewis. *Conrad Celtis: The German Arch-Humanist*. Cambridge, Mass., 1957.

Stokes, Francis Griffin. *Epistolae Obscurorum Virorum.* London, 1909.
Strauß, David Friedrich. *Ulrich von Hutten,* ed. Karl Martin Schiller. Meersburg and Leipzig, 1930.
Szamatolski, Siegfried. *Ulrichs von Hutten deutsche Schriften,* Quellen und Forschungen zur Sprach- und Culturgeschichte der germanischen Völker, vol. 67. Straßburg, 1891.
Worcester, David. *The Art of Satire.* New York, 1960.

INDEX

Adriatic, 45
Aeneas Sylvius (Enea Silvio Piccolomini), Italian humanist and pope (Pius II), 56, 67
    De curialium miseriis, 56
Albrecht von Mainz, archbishop and cardinal, 23, 25, 29, 53, 78, 79, 82, 93
d'Alviano, Bartolomeo, Venetian commander, 44, 74
Amerbach, Bonifatius, Basel humanist and jurist, 24, 92
Anjou, 90
Anshelm, Thomas, printer in Hagenau, 48-49
Aristotle, 26
Bamberg, 15
Basel, 25
Bavaria, 59
Beatus Rhenanus (Beat Bild aus Rheinau), Basel and Schlettstadt humanist and historian, 80, 81
Behaim, Laurenz, Bamberg canon, 9, 10, 18, 19
Bologna, 10-13, 14, 20, 21, 49, 81
Budé, Guillaume, French humanist, 25, 81
Busche, Hermann von dem, Cologne humanist, 14, 17, 18, 48, 50, 91, 92
Cajetan, Thomas de Vio, cardinal and papal legate, 35, 42, 62-64
Camerarius, Joachim, humanist and teacher, 47
Capnion, see "Reuchlin"
Celtis, Konrad (Pickel), humanist poet, 64
Charles V, 70, 89
Cochlaeus, Johann (Dobneck aus Wendelstein), humanist and, from 1520 on, defender of Roman Catholicism, 10, 11, 13, 14
Cologne, 19, 50, 92
Coppus, Gregor, physician to Albrecht von Mainz, 25
Crocus, Richard (Croke), English humanist who taught Greek at Louvain, Cologne, and Leipzig, 8
Crotus Rubeanus (Johann Jäger aus Dornheim), leading author of the *Eov*, 2-4, 6, 8, 14-18, 27
Dante Alighieri, 89
    "Inferno," 89

INDEX

Delos, island in the Aegean, seat of an oracle of Apollo, 51
Democritus, 17
Dodona in Epirus, location of a shrine of Zeus, 51
Eberbach, Peter, humanist from Erfurt, 26
Eccius dedolatus, humanist satire on Johann Eck, 1520, 88
England, 7
Epistolae obscurorum virorum (*Eov*), 1-21, 23, 47, 50, 55, 77, 84
Erasmus of Rotterdam, 6-8, 10, 23, 25, 37, 38, 48-50, 56, 66, 78, 81, 90, 91, 93
    Diversoria, 93
    Encomium moriae, 66
    Ichthyophagia, 90
    Spongia adversus aspergines Hutteni, 48, 91
Exurge domine, papal bull of June 15, 1520, threatening Luther and others with excommunication, 27, 34
Fachus, Balthasar (Fabricius aus Vacha an der Werra), humanist pedagogue, 24, 87
Fischer, Friedrich, Würzburg canon, 30, 85
France, 7, 37, 44, 80
Frankfurt am Main, 91
Froben, Johann, Basel printer and humanist, 37, 56
Fuchs, Jakob, Würzburg canon, 15, 17, 18, 28, 85
Fuggers, the, Augsburg financiers, 42, 69, 71
Gerbel, Nikolaus, Straßburg humanist, 11-14, 20, 50, 54
Germany, 1, 10-12, 27, 46, 49, 60, 61, 63, 65, 81
Glauburg, Arnold von, Frankfurt jurist, 30, 71
Glauburg, Kunigunde von, a relation of Arnold von Glauburg, 30
Gratius, Ortvinus (de Graes), quasi-humanist of Cologne, 10, 16, 19, 52
Hagenau, 48-49
Herder, Johann Gottfried, 1
Hessus, Eoban (Koch aus Bockendorf in Hessen), humanist poet, 26, 47, 89, 91, 95
Hitler, Adolf, 1
Hochstraten, Jakob, Cologne inquisitor, 19, 20, 48, 50, 52, 78, 92

INDEX

Homer, 90
Hutten, Agapetus von, 34
Hutten, Hans von, 33, 59-61
Hutten, Ludwig von, Hans von Hutten's father, 59, 60
Hutten, Ludwig von, Hans von Hutten's brother, 34
Hutten, Ulrich von
    Ad Caesarem Maximilianum epigrammatum liber, 44-45, 64, 91
    Ad Caesarem Maximilianum ut bellum in Venetos coeptum prosequatur exhortatorium, 46-47
    "Ad poetas Germanos," from *In Lossios querelarum liber secundus*, 11-13
    Ad principes Germanos ut bellum Turcis inferant exhortatoria (*Türkenrede*), 78
    Aula, 29, 35, 36, 53-56, 58, 64, 92-93
    Beklagunge der Freistette deutscher nation, 41
    Bulla, 27, 56-58, 64
    De Guaiaci medicina et morbo Gallico, 24
    De piscatura Venetorum, 45-47, 64
    De statu Romano, 33
    De unitate ecclesiae conservanda and preface, 79, 95
    Epistola ad Maximilianum Caesarem, Italiae ficticia, 13, 76-77
    Expostulatio cum Erasmo, 6-7
    Febris I, 26, 41-43
    Febris II, 41-43, 65, 71-72, 74
    Fortuna, 36, 65-72, 74, 79
    In annum M.D. XVI. prognosticon ad Leonem X. Pont. Max., 77
    In laudem Alberti Archiepiscopi Moguntini panegyricus, 24
    In Lossios querelarum liber secundus, 11
    In sceleratissimam Ioannis Pepericorni vitam exclamatio, 55
    Inspicientes, 35, 57, 62-64
    In tempora Iulii satyra, 32
    "Liberis omnibus ac vere Germanis," 78-79, 82
    Marcus, 44-46, 63, 91

Monitor II, 64
Nemo, 2, 4, 27-28, 37-41, 43, 73, 74, 88-90
Phalarismus, 33, 52, 55, 58-65
Praedones, 35, 55, 65
Triumphus Capnionis, 47-53, 58, 62, 64, 78, 85, 91-92
Türkenrede, see *Ad principes Germanos... exhortatoria*
Vadiscus, 26, 79
Italy, 20, 25, 27, 44, 81
Julius II, 32, 77
Juvenal, 67-68, 71
    Tenth Satire, 67-68
Lange, Johann, Erfurt teacher and friar, 47
Latium, used as equivalent to "Italy," *q.v.*
Lefèvre d'Étaples, Jacques, French humanist, 25-26
Leo X, 34, 57, 71, 76-80, 82, 95
Lucian, 1, 66, 67, 87
    The Dream, 67
    The Ship, 67
Luther, Martin, 34
Mainz, 29, 80, 91
Maximilian I, 13, 59, 76, 77
Medici, the, 77
Melanchthon, Philip (Schwarzert), Wittenberg professor and reformer, 47
Menapius, Gulielmus, Aachen canon, 92-93
    Aula, 92
Menius, Justus, Lutheran humanist, translator of Naogeorg's *Pammachius*, 2, 3, 6, 16-17
Meyer, Peter, Frankfurt parson, 52-53
Munich, 40
Murner, Thomas, 12
Mutianus Rufus (Konrad Muth), Gotha canon, 26, 48, 50, 91
Naumburg, Bertram von, Mainz clergyman, 52
Neuenar, Hermann von, Cologne canon, 92
Nürnberg, 77

INDEX

Oecolampadius, Johann (Hüsgen), Basel reformer, 25, 37
Paris, 80, 81
Pavia, 24
Petrarch, 66
    De remediis utriusque fortunae, 66
Peutinger, Konrad, Augsburg humanist, 29
Pfefferkorn, Johann, initiator of the controversy with Reuchlin over the confiscation of Hebrew books in Germany, 51
Pforzheim, 51
Pirckheimer, Wilibald, Nürnberg humanist, 9-11, 13, 18, 19, 23, 25, 29, 37, 49, 76-78, 81, 88
Plato, 35
Plautus, 88
    Casina, 88
Rabstein, Prokop von, Bohemian friend of Aeneas Sylvius at the court of Emperor Friedrich III, 67
Radulfus, French monk of the thirteenth century, 89-90
Reuchlin, Johann (Capnion), Swabian humanist and Hebraist, 12, 15, 16, 47-48, 50, 51, 78, 91, 92
Rome, 20, 33, 42, 46, 76, 92
Sabine, wife of Ulrich, Duke of Württemberg, 59
Schan, Jörg, author of a version of the "Nemo"-idea, 89-90
Sermo pauperis Henrici de sancto Nemine, a version of the "Nemo"-idea, 90
Sickingen, Franz von, German condottiere and protector of Hutten, 23, 35, 57, 65
Steckelberg, fortress of the Huttens, near Fulda, 70, 80, 81
Stein, Eitelwolf vom, humanist and statesman in the service of Albrecht von Mainz, 24, 28
Straßburg, 12, 89
Streitberg, Georg von, jurist, friend of Hutten, 29
Stromer, Heinrich, physician from Augsburg, builder of the Auerbach Hof, 29, 36
Swift, Jonathan, 74
Tabula Cebetis, late Hellenic allegory on the life of man, 66
Tungern, Arnold von, Cologne theologian, 19, 52

INDEX

Ulrich, Duke of Württemberg, 33, 59-63, 65, 88
Urban, Heinrich, Cistercian in Erfurt, 91
Valla, Lorenzo, Italian humanist, 76, 79, 95
    De donatione Constantini, 76, 78-80, 82, 95
Venice, 44, 45
Zehender, Bartholomeus, parson in Mainz, 52
Zonarius, Fabius (Gürtler), humanist from Goldberg in
    Silesia, 19
Zwingli, Ulrich, Zürich reformer, 80

www.ingramcontent.com/pod-product-compliance
Lightning Source LLC
Chambersburg PA
CBHW031321150426
43191CB00005B/276